AN INTRODUCTION
TO
YACHT DESIGN

BY

A. A. SYMONDS

PREFACE

In 1921 I built my first boat. She was a flat-bottomed punt, built mostly by guess and by grace, but no less successful for this if judged by the river miles covered with pole and sail. The local boat-builder was kind— boat-builders, I have noticed, are quite astonishingly kind in the way they talk about their art—and thereupon began for me the intriguing study of ships and their manner of going. It was not long before I had redesigned my punt in the light of incipient knowledge and experience.

Thus it is with most of us who acquire a boat. Sooner or later we become inveterate critics. There is something about boats that induces curiosity in matters nautical and provokes discussions of technicalities, and even deep reading on the subject. Shortly my drawing-board recorded ideas for a more thoroughbred sailing craft, and although some years passed before I found time personally to build a dinghy to my own design, *Naval Architecture* had taken a place on my bookshelf. The rest was natural ; the course is set for I know not what, but in the meantime it has brought me a real little cruiser of my own.

So far as Yacht Architecture is concerned, it is as an amateur that I have read, and from this point of view, while finding a lot written for the inexperienced in scattered pages of periodicals, I have found no handy volume with the more outstanding features of yacht design collected for those whose interest is just beginning. As such a book I hope this will be found attractive.

I am learning almost every time I sail or watch a boat take shape in a builder's shed, and so will all those who presume to study the way of a ship in the midst of the sea. Hence there are blank pages included in these notes for readers' own observations on this most alluring of pastimes. Risking the obvious gibe, I particularly commend these blank pages to their service.

A. A. S.

CONTENTS

LIST OF DIAGRAMS

8

PART I

THEORY AND CONSTRUCTION

I

CERTAIN LAWS OF HYDROSTATICS, AND CONVENTIONS USED IN THE DRAWING OF YACHTS

All the world knows the plain fact that wood floats, yet to the uninitiated it must seem rather optimistic that a designer can hang on huge chunks of iron or lead and still be confident that his ship will float when she is launched. The fact is that water pushes heavily against the sides of any tank containing it, and likewise against the sides of anything immersed in it. In still water at any given level below the surface the pressure is everywhere the same, pushing against everything it finds there with a pressure per square inch equal to the weight of water in a tube, of one square inch cross-section, reaching from the level in question to the surface. This sounds involved, but the result is astonishingly simple. If a certain volume of anything is immersed in water, the water exerts on it a lifting force equal in amount to the weight of an equal volume of water. If anything is only partly immersed the lifting force is the weight of water equal in volume to the immersed part only ; and for a boat this force obviously supports the boat. For a floating ship the whole weight, hull, sails, and gear, is supported by a lifting force equal to the weight of water displaced by the immersed part of the hull. If one adds 100 pounds of gear to a boat she sinks lower in the water until the under-water volume of her hull has

9

increased by just that amount which, if filled with water, would weigh 100 pounds. One can go on loading a boat with iron or lead until her total weight is equal to her volume's weight of water ; after that she will sink.

Sea water takes 35 cubic feet to the ton, so that a yacht with an under-water body of 350 cubic feet weighs 10 tons. This sort of problem often turns up, but fortunately it is an easy one.

The under-water volume of a yacht is called her displacement; and this volume immediately gives her total weight which is so important a matter to the designer, besides giving to all interested an idea of the boat's size, that the displacement is generally stated in tons of water displaced rather than in cubic feet.

This Displacement Tonnage must not be confused with Thames Measurement tonnage, which latter is found by putting certain of the ship's dimensions into a formula ; on being worked out this gives the weight very roughly. The formula will be found on page 123.

Another important law is that the upward lift of the water, the force supporting a floating boat, acts through the centre of gravity of the under-water volume of the boat. This centre of gravity is called the centre of buoyancy—the C.B.—of a boat, and a designer needs must know where it is in order to get the ballast keel in the right place if for no other reason ; if the downward weight of the hull is not vertically in line with the supporting force of the water the boat will tilt like a pair of scales. Fig. 1 shows the effect of a lead keel put in the wrong place, and needs no explanation.

Builders and sailing men are mostly conservative, and boats will long continue to be built of wood in the manner established by years of boat-building experience.

A totally new method of construction may be invented
—steel hulls have arrived for instance—but as the life
of a properly built hull should be thirty years or more
it will be long hence before revolutionary ideas can be
thoroughly proved and usurp the place of existing
practice.

Laws of Nature are even more abiding. They
have always been involved in the building of ships, and
when we delight in the individuality of a ship responding
to the tiller in our hand it is due to some fine blending
of their invariable effects ; in these days we can learn

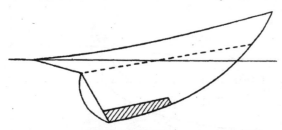

FIG. 1.—Effect of wrongly placed ballast.

something of it by pondering the drawings, for although
the reality is wrought in wood it was conceived on paper
and is recorded.   Often, too, designs get no further than
the paper, but even so they are things for fascinating
speculation—Is she fast ? How will she handle ?
What will she cost ?

There is nothing difficult in reading drawings, but
speedy comprehension only follows practice. " Lines "
are geometrical drawings showing the hull form from
three aspects, without regard to perspective, while the
accommodation and construction drawings are in the
nature of mechanical drawings.   Lines are no mysterious
property of boats alone. Any block may be said to

11

have lines, and for a boat they are the outlines of slices
through the hull. Fig. 2 may be helpful, as the lines
are there reduced to a minimum. In the upper sketch
is the outline of the ship's elevation seen from one side,

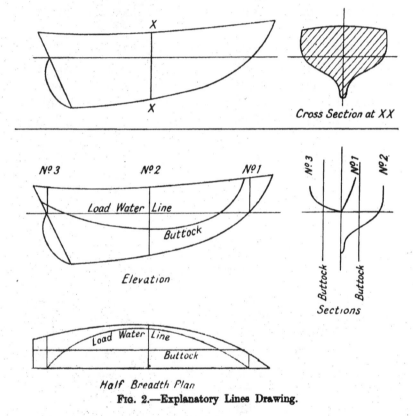

Fig. 2.—Explanatory Lines Drawing.

and to the right of it the outline of the hull if cut across
amidships; this outline is called a section. Naturally
sections can be drawn for other cuts besides that amidships, and when any section is drawn the position of the
cut is marked on the elevation by a vertical line. In

the lower sketch a group of three sections appears, half only for the two sides are alike, and to distinguish them each section is numbered and its position on the elevation marked by a line numbered likewise.

In the same way a cut parallel to the water surface seen from above gives a curved outline called a water line, and such a cut made exactly at the surface is called the Load Water Line, or L.W.L. This curve is shown on the half breadth plan drawn below the elevation, and the position of the cut marked by a straight horizontal line on the elevation and sections.

A fore-and-aft vertical cut parallel to the ship's centre line but to one side of it is called a buttock ; and the position of this cut is marked by a straight line on the plan showing the water line, and by two straight lines on the sections, for, as only half sections are drawn, some are on one side and some are on the other side of the axis.

Slanting fore-and-aft cuts called diagonals are another group of curves generally shown below the water lines. Their positions are marked on the sections by straight lines at an angle to the vertical axis. Two diagonals are shown in fig. 3.

In addition to these the deck level is drawn, whose upward curve from stern to stem is called the sheer ; and in transom sterned yachts the apparent form of a raking transom as seen from astern, from which view the more important actual shape is derived. Generally too, the position of the wood keel is marked on the elevation as it enables the actual shape to be found. The business of getting the actual shape of sloping parts requires a certain cunning, but as a pastime it is more intriguing than crosswords.

13

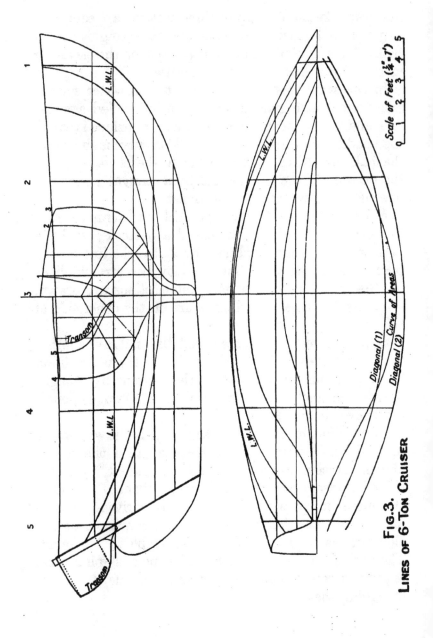

FIG. 3.
LINES OF 6-TON CRUISER

Scale of Feet (¾"=1')
0   1   2   3   4   5

L.W.L.

Transom

Transom

L.W.L.

L.W.L.

L.W.L.

Diagonal (1)
Curve of Areas
Diagonal (2)

A rather more complete set of lines is given in fig. 3, but the water lines, sections, and buttocks are scanty to avoid confusion. It is usual to divide the load water line into ten or twelve spaces and to draw in some six water lines, but this is by no means a rigid rule.

The conventions of mechanical drawing are used to portray the interior of a ship. The elevation drawings showing the accommodation and construction are a view of the hull as if sliced vertically down the fore-and-aft centre line ; whatever would then be disclosed is drawn in to scale. Dotted lines represent concealed things that would not really be disclosed by such a view, while shaded spaces between the lines show that the slice would there be cutting through solid material.

II

SPEED, ACCOMMODATION, AND COST

One can argue for ever as to what is the best boat. Comfort, speed, cost, and beauty, figure in any opinion, and which of these is adjudged the most important depends only on one's own ideas. Nevertheless, comfort is the nucleus of design, and the number for whom it has to be provided, for one cannot get bathrooms into a five-tonner any more than one can get quarts into a pint pot. It is surprising, though, what discomforts are unheeded afloat, and a little ship of 2 tons can be very fast if no more than creeping headroom is required.

Speed is a common desire, possessed even by those who maintain that a fast boat cannot be a comfortable boat and that no genuine cruiser can be fast; yet touching speed it is safe only to say that a ship will please her owner if she makes fast passages, and that for anything short of a houseboat a designer will have to build speed as effectively as he can around the demanded interior.

A dinghy for fishing is not built exactly as the latest 14-foot international, although a 14-foot dinghy might be admirably suited for fishing. For this it has to provide seats and lockers, etc., for the convenience of the fisherman and his gear; but if the cost might reach the £150 level without protest from the purchaser, the dinghy would without doubt be very fast, a work of art differing externally from the thoroughbred racer by an inch or two of freeboard and a foot or two of sail area. In actual fact the fishing enthusiast, having stated demands calling for a liner, would end up with the remark, " She must not cost more than £30."

Poverty is a real distinction, and it is no use attempting a class of ship one cannot afford. A poor man takes pride in a fast boat like everyone else, and gets his fun racing his £30 boat in a handicap on form class where it does not matter if the plate is polished bronze or not.

Often enough the accommodation demanded as absolutely essential and the price that can be found have so little in common as to spoil the ship, and it is up to designers to avert this tragedy.

Standard Designs.

Naturally cost and size increase together, but if certain features are reproduced in a number of hulls it enables a considerable amount of preliminary work to do for the lot, so effecting a considerable saving in cost. Such a process is distantly akin to mass production as found in the car industry, but not carried to such carefully considered extremes.

Standard designs offer a great deal to those who prize possession of a real ship above a design peculiar to themselves, and the list on page 18 shows what can be got for one's money in the way of a new cruising yacht.[1] It shows the accommodation, size, and cost of various yachts built in competition with each other to please that great number of sailing people who have to get as much ship as possible for a small favourable

[1] Other standard designs exist; these are only representative.

SOME STANDARD CRUISERS

Builder	L.O.A.	L.W.L.	Beam	Draft	Sail Area	Tonnage T.M.	Accommodation [1]	Cost [2]
David Hillyard (Littlehampton)	18'	16' 6"	6' 6"	3'	175	2·6	2	£125
	21'	19' 6"	7'	3' 6"	224	3·6	2	£175
Mashford Bros. (Plymouth)	20'	18'	7'	4'	240	3·4	2 with 4 H.P. engine	£202 10s.
	23'	as above but with canoe stern						£222 10s.
Sharp & Penn (Woodbridge)	20' 6"	18' 6"	7' 9"	3' 6"	268	4·1	2	£175
	23'	21'	8' 3"	3' 10"	330	5·3	2 to 3	£245
	28'	24' 9"	8' 4"	4' 8"	490	7·4	4	£415
Dan Webb (Maldon)	20' 3"	18'	6' 9"	3' 6"	230	3·3	2	£178 10s.

[1] In most boats alternative accommodation is offered.
[2] November, 1937.

18

balance at the bank. The price of cruisers is for the complete yacht, and generally includes some form of ground tackle.

Clearly there is a general opinion that £125 is the lowest cost to give habitable accommodation for two, and this in a yacht of about 17 feet on the water line. Smaller ships might be cheaper, but their disadvantages would be out of all proportion. £125 is a lot of money, but one gets something invaluable for it; and if none of these designs brings forth sounds of pleasure from one who is burning with sea fever the unresponsive individual must be lacking in imagination, or else more concerned with aerodynamics or teak panelling than with seafaring.

In the smallest cruisers, the 18-foot overall yachts, the cockpits are about 3 feet 6 inches in length, and the cabins at least 6 feet with sitting headroom under the coach-roof beams. This allows for two full-length settee berths and some 20 inches of floor space between. A small corner screened off for a galley and sundry lockers are general features, with a fore peak or fo'c'sle as a useful store; a fore hatch is, as a rule, a small extra. A simple finish and straightforward layout are to be expected, but in many ways yachts are finished to please individual purchasers.

As cruisers they are fit in every way for a summer cruise, but it must be admitted that if weather bound for long even larger boats seem to shrink in internal dimensions. Whether the next size larger, the four-tonner, is regarded as providing more comfort for two or insufficient comfort for three is a matter of choice, for a pipe cot can just be squeezed into the fo'c'sle. The price has risen of course, but so has the water-line

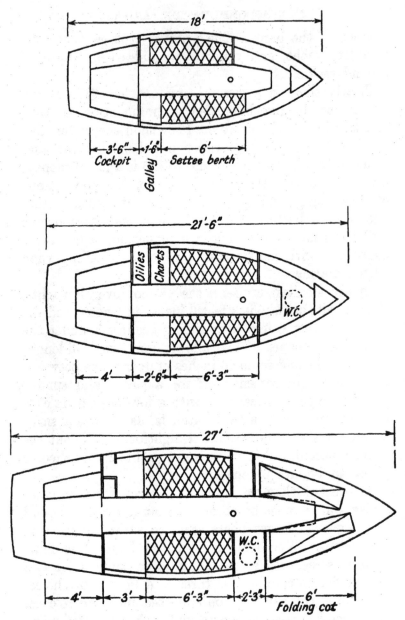

FIG. 4.—Comparison of Accommodation.

20

length and sail area ; one has a larger, faster and more comfortable boat in fact.

Between 4 and 6 tons an inordinate jump seems to occur in the important matter of cost. Four as a crew are possible, and bunks for four mean room for two end on, at least 1·2 feet for sleeping, with stowage for their gear and for the equipment of a larger ship.

Fig. 4 shows the increasing accommodation possible with increasing size of ship ; the layouts being of comparative rather than practical merit.

General Features Inboard

Sailing boats vary from J class to dinghies, and for the small boat man it is his choice of inboard comfort that really settles his choice of yacht. But comfort afloat is not predictable from household experience only.

Below decks sitting comfort is important, but not always present. Sitting headroom requires a clear 3 feet above the settee cushions, and if the side decks are not high enough to allow this headroom the space beneath them must be packed out inside (with lockers, etc.) from hull topsides to cabin coamings so as to support one's back and shoulders ; otherwise, on leaning back one's head will fetch up against the coamings. Short or tall mankind requires 3 feet for sitting.

Six-foot headroom, however, is a lure for the unwary. It sounds well and appeals to the armchair critic ; but we all bump our heads somewhere in any ship until we get familiar with its hard corners, and the cabin roof is the least likely place to catch us unawares. Six-foot headroom in a small boat means an excessively high coach roof ; and with less than 23 feet of

. water line one should be content to stretch in the cockpit.

Luxury increases with size, until, at the moment, it stops short with the *Queen Mary*. Here we draw the line at 7 tons or thereabouts, and on a water line of 25 feet to 28 feet the designer's job is to lay out luxury for two as it may be reckoned in small boats, or to find space for four.

In a modern seven-tonner a separate compartment for a galley and again for a lavatory are found, and there are alternative positions for these. Most people find the galley is best placed just inside the cabin where motion at sea is less violent than up forward ; but with a paid hand aboard the galley is naturally forward of the saloon bulkhead, sometimes in the fo'c'sle, sometimes in a separately partitioned space. The latter has advantages, but the separate space in a seven-tonner is generally so small that a corner of the fo'c'sle is preferable. Here the cook can at times spread his wares on benches normally intended for other uses, a great thing when washing up. Lamps and paraffin, etc., can be stored up there too, putting the primus and cooking and other messy things all together. But wherever the galley is, see that the pantry is within easy reach, and the water tank not very far away.

A separately housed lavatory needs good headroom for washing and trouser work, which puts it somewhere under the coach roof of anything under 7 tons, and this compartment is often found just inside the cabin. This site, though, seems to waste a large chunk of the best part of the ship's interior for business which does not take much of the day. However, it is all a matter of opinion. Putting something just inside the companion-way pushes the saloon forward and helps to keep it dry.

The air draft in a small ship is from aft forward when the fore hatch is open, a very relevant fact when planning galleys and lavatories.

Big yachts are not always the most original. Amongst smaller boats I once found a noteworthy 19-foot cutter rigged out for the owner's solitary cruising ; one low settee was to port with a folding cot above, which, bulging with bedding inside, made a cushion for his back as he sat below ; the galley was just inside to starboard, and beyond this a table, bookshelf, chart-rack, and lockers that would have been commodious on a six-tonner. There was half a bulkhead only by the mast making the small space beyond more accessible, and yet the saloon possessed an elegance altogether absent when there is no fore bulkhead at all. The cockpit, too, seemed roomy for so small a ship, and yet somehow covered a marine engine. It was no good ship for mixed bathing parties.

With 20 feet of water line if there is no need for a pipe cot in the fo'c'sle the forward bulkhead can be pushed forward, leaving space for indulging in fancies, a larger cockpit for day sailing or more locker and galley space for serious cruising. An oilskin locker just inside the companion-way is doubly valuable because the oilies are to hand when required and they can be stowed away again before dripping water over everything below.

Pull-down berths take up a little more room than berths made up on a settee unless their hinges are arranged on a line parallel with the centre line of the hull, which is not always possible. Sometimes to overcome this difficulty the bulkheads are skewed to bring them at right angles to whatever line the bunks may hinge on, but this introduces its own difficulties. Another method is to have the bunks shaped to fit the hull, like pipe cots, but this is not very sightly and somewhere reduces the size of the bunk. It must be admitted that pull-down bunks are a joy when turning in and blanket work is to the fore—but when putting them into the drawing remember that when folded up the ends of the bunks are closer to the hull than the centre part, and it behoves one to think out the necessary clearance for blankets between the bunk-ends and the hull timbers.

Chart tables are a valued but difficult achievement on a small yacht. The usual all-purpose folding table stands in the middle of the saloon floor and is very much in the way besides being an unstable invention. An area 3 feet by 2 feet is not easily obtained, however, and a table worth considering is one pulling down athwartships from behind the saloon settees. Such a table can be made to contain a chart-rack wherein charts may be stowed flat, but if there is no room for this, a rack long enough to take the longest rolled-up chart can be fitted against the hull side, piercing if need be one of the bulkheads.

Unless there is adequate headroom under the cabin top beams there is no object in putting a w.c. there, and a better place is in the bows in such a position that one has standing room with the fore hatch open.

A common place for stowing things is in lockers under the settees and fo'c'sle benches, but builders delight in fitting exasperatingly small entrances by way of the top ; insist on a big hole wherever it is. With high and wide seats the lockers beneath can have a hinged door in front which saves cushion-lifting when thirsty, for these lockers always seem to be the cellar. Lockers in general should open fore and aft, not athwartships, for a boat heels to a greater angle than she pitches and things are thrown out athwartships more readily than fore and aft.

It does not take a skilled designer to see that a beamy deep drafted boat has more interior than a narrow and shallow one ; but note that it is in a way that affects headroom and general roominess rather than the number of crew the ship can sleep. Beam and draft have to be paid for too, so that experience keeps them within fairly well-defined limits depending on the length of the ship.

Locality, too, has a say in the matter of draft. On the east and south coasts as far west as Poole, the shallow water of the harbours and harbour bars calls for shallow draft as a local requirement, and 5 feet is as much as is wanted, with an effort apparent to keep it down to 3 feet 6 inches or so in the smaller cruisers. At first glance this might seem to challenge the prior claim of accommodation on the designer, but as in shallow draft yachts high and wide cabin-tops are general for the clear reason of obtaining space, while in deep draft yachts flush decks are commonly found, the importance of accommodation is maintained.

Once racing and super windward ability no longer feature in the dreamer's ideals, he can encompass his perfect ship by an easier and less expensive hull. This is a very sound outlook when nothing more than leisurely cruising is in view, but the engine room becomes emphatically important.

There are so many engines of all sizes and shapes

. 25

that one can be found to fit almost any part of any ship, and in consequence the space allotted to them often suggests practical ignorance or worse on the part of the designer. If you are going to trust your engine to get you out of one place and into another, not to mention out of a mess, put it somewhere where neglect is not excusable on account of inaccessibility. The cockpit may be a useful engine-room roof, but it is a rotten engine-room door. When tinkering with the engine it is as important to keep out rain and driven spray as to let in the spanners of a mechanic.

III

HULL FORM AND ITS BEARING ON SPEED

This sailing business has come to us as a sport after centuries of existence as a means of livelihood, years in which the old order of seafarers and shipwrights developed a ship of such perfect form and construction that men could rely on it even in gales. Yet from a scientific point of view the best form of hull shape remains something of a mystery and hull design an art rather than a science.

Whatever the ship, she will please her owner if she makes fast passages, and this has provoked much searching into the causes of the various forms of drag that retard a ship moving through the water. Friction, water eddies, and surface waves dominate amongst enemies of speed afloat, of which only friction can be computed with any degree of certainty.

Friction ashore is well understood, and if the arch enemy of motion, at least it does not depend on the speed with which one thing slides over another, nor on the area of the surface in contact between them; but afloat the frictional drag between ship and water depends on the speed of the ship and on the area of her surface immersed in the water. Hence the cutaway fore foot and raked sternpost of racing yachts, for not only do they make a boat handy but they contribute to speed by reducing deadwood and surface area to a minimum. Compare the hulls of fig. 5. The triangular profile may have 25 per cent. less area immersed than the straight stemmer. Off the wind the centre plates of dinghies can be run up into their cases to keep them out of the water altogether.

To a small extent also the shape affects the frictional drag, a long shallow form having rather less friction than a short deep one of the same area. It is interesting, though, that so long as the surface is smooth it does not matter much what coating is put on, but weeds or barnacles or any roughness whatever increase the drag and warrant the use of the most effective antifouling one can find.

Fig. 5.—Hull comparison.

Streamlines

Deep down in the sea fishes and submarines move through the water without a ripple showing on the surface; it is when moving on the surface that their progress is marked by waves. In submerged movement resistance to motion is due to eddies forming at corners and bumps on the submarine, and to reduce these eddies special shapes have been tried. The so-called streamline shape, blunt nose and tapering tail, is the natural path one drop of water would follow on meeting the submerged form deep down in the ocean.

It is easier to think of a stationary form and a current of water flowing past it. Then, if one drop follows a particular path round an obstacle all other drops immediately behind it follow the same path one after the other, and we get the idea of a line of drops streaming away round the stationary form—streamlines in fact. Watch the tide swirling past a buoy ; close in there is a turbulent lot of eddies, while further from the buoy the water slides smoothly past on either side and joins up again astern of it. Were the buoy shaped like the path of the smoothly flowing water outside the eddies, there would be no turbulent eddy-filled area around the buoy. The buoy would be streamlined.

Deep down the same thing is happening, and when an odd-shaped thing is moving through still water the eddies formed about it mean so much energy put into the water ; the eddies actually warm the water slightly as they die away. This energy lost in the water means additional drag on a moving boat, and as in any fluid, be it air or water, the well-known streamline shape is found to move most easily, the well-submerged part of a boat should be streamlined as far as possible.

Waves.

It is well known that the maximum speed a boat will attain unless driven by inordinately powerful engines depends on her water-line length ; and in any but very light craft experience shows the maximum speed in knots (sea miles per hour) does not much exceed $1\frac{1}{4}$ times the square root of the water line in feet. The much greater speeds of lighter craft are due to planing, a state in which the boat is lifted out of the water to skim along the surface like a surf-riding board behind a speed-boat.

Speed in knots is numerically some 15 per cent less than when measured in statute miles per hour. One knot is one sea mile per hour; and one sea mile is 2,027 yards, whereas the statute mile is 1,760 yards.

The extraordinary importance of length is known to arise from the formation of waves which arise in addition to eddies when things move on the surface of water, and which at high speeds are a more serious drag.

Any waves on the surface of the sea are started by a force of some sort and gradually subside if no sustaining force keeps them going. A motor-boat driven fast starts a welter of waves which arises continuously from

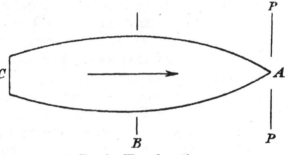

FIG. 6.—Wave formation.

it and spreads out behind as it moves along; and this wave-making is a drag on the boat the propulsive force of the engines is overcoming.

About the middle of the last century Colin Archer elaborated a theory for minimizing this wave resistance. The displaced volume of a yacht is contained within the yacht's water-line length and he argued that this volume should be distributed along the length of the water line in the same proportion that the volume of a wave on the sea is distributed between trough and trough; thus the theoretical wave shapes of versed sine and trochoid became of interest, curves one occasionally finds amongst the lines of a yacht. However, nothing was really known until Froude made a careful study of resistance to motion and a ship's length and speed.

In fig. 6 a ship is supposed to be approaching a line PP on the surface of the water. As her bows approach the line they begin pushing the water at PP aside, piling it up on either side of the ship as she passes. Then owing to intricate changes of pressure the water falls to its old level and below, and so begins a motion like a weight heaving on the end of a spring. The water at PP heaves up and down while the ship moves on, piling up the water at her bows and continuously starting a wave motion which thus appears to be moving with the ship.

Now her stern is doing just the same. A second wave is started at PP soon after the midship section B arrives there. This leaves behind a second heaving up and down, and when the line PP is left astern of the ship there are two independent upheavals going on—one due to the entry between A and B, and the other due to the run between B and C.

If now one of these motions left astern of the ship at PP is upwards at the same moment that the other is downwards, the resulting motion is nothing much and the boat leaves a clean wake; while if both motions at PP are upwards together there is a hell of a wave. Whether the two waves come together or cancel out depends on the ship's length and speed, for the bows A must move on a distance AB before the run BC can start wave-making at PP.

At very slow speeds no appreciable waves are formed, and when they do begin they more or less cancel out astern but show a most conspicuous wave hollow along the weather side of a sailing ship as in fig. 7. A little faster and so vigorous does the wave formation become that large waves pile up astern.

Waves, we have seen, mean drag on a boat, a drag that increases so rapidly with speed that it practically settles the maximum speed a sailing yacht can reach ; and this wave-making propensity of boats becomes prominent when their speed in knots is about $1\frac{1}{4}$ times the square root of the water line in feet. Thus it comes about that length is said to determine a yacht's maximum speed.

Note carefully that although the waves on the surface

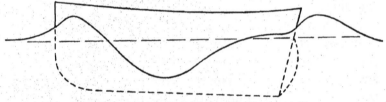

FIG. 7.—Profile of wave alongside yacht (exaggerated).

of the sea appear to be moving bodily along, the water itself is only moving up and down or very nearly so. This effect is well shown by waves on a long length of rope when one end is shaken up and down.

Waves are far more complicated than the above outline suggests, and the precise nature of waves raised by ships has long defied mathematicians although the theoretical waves from certain ship-like forms have been calculated. Mr. W. C. S. Wigley [1] has given an instructive analysis of the waves from a deep-drafted ship with parabolic water lines, and although real ships certainly have a different shape the results are of great

[1] *Proc. Roy. Soc.*, Vol. 144, March, 1934.

interest and show for this model the existence of six different wave systems, two at the bows, two at the stern, and two more amidships at either end of a short parallel body into which the curved water lines merged. The two bow waves spring one from the angle of entry and one from the curvature of the water lines, and the two waves from the run come similarly; while those amidships are due to the change in shape caused by the parallel body. These last are in general small and in any case will not concern a normal sailing yacht.

The resistance due to these theoretical waves is calculable. Waves from the angle of entry cause a resistance that increases as the square of the speed, while waves from the water-line curvature cause a resistance that increases as the fourth power of the speed ; meanwhile interference or combination effects between different waves further complicates the matter.

IV

HULL FORM

The form of all modern yachts has unquestionably felt the influence of racing developments, and for the most part to their benefit in spite of those aspects of debatable seaworthiness.

There are two forms of racing, one design racing and handicap racing. One designs, lest anyone is not clear as to the significance of the term, are in theory exactly similar boats so that the racing tests skill and helmsmanship; handicaps by one means or another attempt to amend actual finishing times so that slower or smaller boats have a fair chance of finishing first. Class rules and restrictions are a popular way of compromise, seeking to encourage experiment in design while tying the designer to a boat that will be compatible with others in the class. To hundreds who love trying out new ideas these are a natural delight, particularly in the dinghy world, where their existence from drawing board to actual racing can be tackled by an amateur.

Where a class rule has determined hull form development shows a rather cramped style. Whereas a bad rule will certainly produce undesirable developments a good rule does not always produce good developments, for it is certain that yacht designers are better at circumventing rules than committees at making them. A simple example of rule dodging is in the measurement

34

of a yacht's water-line length, for it is this that largely
determines a boat's speed. In anything of a breeze
yachts sail heeled over so that the water line at, say,
15 degrees is the length that counts, and a cunning
designer can make this greater than the upright water
line which was the basis of many rules.

Length, Beam, and Draft

Length is the foundation of a free design. It settles
a boat's size and speed to a preliminary inquiry, and
although if either beam or draft vanished so would the
boat, the latter two are complementary to length and
need be sufficient only to provide adequate stiffness for
sail-carrying.

There is no clear-cut optimum beam for a boat, and
its limits are set on the large side by uneasy motion
and on the small side by lack of stiffness or righting
effort. From current practice one may say that if
the beam gets far from the purely empirical value
$\frac{L}{4} + 2\frac{1}{4}$ feet (where L is the water-line length) the boat
is a bit of a freak. However, in small cruisers roominess
below is often of sufficient importance to justify beam
to an extent racing folk call tubbiness.

In a general way draft makes for windward ability,
but one cannot decide on it without taking into account
the home port of the yacht and her cruising or racing
district. From the East Coast to the Solent shallow
creeks and harbour bars put a premium on shallow
draft, which in the limit leads to centre-board boats.

Beam and draft both affect stiffness, but draft and
with it depth of ballast are of less consequence than
beam in a boat which is nearly upright. A point called

35

the metacentre is involved, which point is very much affected by the beam·of a boat, and it is the distance below this point to the centre of gravity of the whole ship that settles the stiffness.

Because a boat is stiff when she is upright, it does not follow that she will be stiff when gun'les under. In shallow-draft boats particularly there is an angle of heel at which stiffness disappears completely, and if a boat reaches this angle she capsizes without more ado. This critical angle is very largely determined by the position

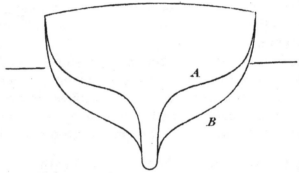

FIG. 8.—Comparison of midship section form.

of the ballast, and, when gun'les under, low-placed lead is most effective in giving a righting moment.

Given a yacht's length the midship section offers more scope to a designer than beam or draft, although the latter are intimately bound to it. In fig. 8 A is a light displacement boat, i.e. one relatively light in weight. This form is good to windward and fast with a very moderate sail plan. Under 2 tons a ship of this section can often be made to plane, skimming the surface at astonishing speeds, and is an ideal form when the interior does not worry the owner. B is the opposite extreme, not necessarily slow but on the same water line would need hard sailing to keep A from vanishing ahead. When it comes to three weeks aboard, though, B has headroom, bunks, lockers, and super cooking equipment.

The greater interior roominess means greater displacement, and as the ship displaces her own weight of water the roomier ship B is inevitably a heavier ship than A. The difference in weight of wood used in construction will not account for the difference in displacement of the two forms, and the roomier ship needs more lead or iron to get her down to her marks.

Profile and Ends.

All modern sailing craft have benefited from the racing stimulant and the profile of modern yachts shows the influence as much as anything. That a surrender to racing practice on this point has not meant sacrificing seaworthiness is proved by the performance at sea of several modern ocean racers and the profile of the famous Gloucester Schooners built for deep-sea fishing. However, good ideas are not proof against abuse, and what is safe for 100 tons is not necessarily safe for a five-tonner. Again, what is safe for a day racing craft may be unseaworthy in a sea-keeping ship.

The more or less triangular profile underwater of modern racing yachts gives another much-prized characteristic, handiness; and the racing hulls of recent years with all their lateral area concentrated, turn with confidence and rapidity. The profile can be cut away till but a narrow fin of lateral area remains, and a yacht will sail perfectly, but a limit to this cutting away is set by the vital necessity of control. To come about with certainty there must be some heel to the lateral area, grip on the water right aft, otherwise, on putting the helm down, the boat comes into the wind and stays there in irons, instead of turning further and sailing off on the other tack. Dinghies sometimes exhibit the oddity of abundant weather helm and yet getting in irons every time they come about. It is cured by moving the centre plate aft or the sails forward.

Cutting away fore foot also cuts away ship, and although in moderation it makes little difference to a nine-tonner, it may mean surrendering the space for a bow model w.c. in a 4-ton yacht. The fo'c'sle of a small yacht is the only sizeable store and sail locker ; inside and outside the bows are important and the best possible use should be made of them. In these days it is fashionable to think of the bows being run out to an overhang which invariably means a scanty fore foot ; and it is a nice point whether the result is a smaller ship at the same price or a larger ship at inordinately increased price.

Concerning the fore foot one hears a lot about fore grip being essential for lying to at sea, and a long keel being essential for steady running. It may be so, but while it is certain that grip on the water helps to keep a boat steady it is not so certain that a well-designed hull needs this help.

The form of the bow and stern sections merges into the question of overhangs and profile. Bow sections may be taken as those from the stem to a little abaft the forward end of the water line, and the section drawn at this end of the water line indicates their form ; likewise the stern sections are delineated in general form by that at the after end of the water line. It is rather obvious that one cannot attain deep narrow

V-shaped sections and at the same time cut away all trace of fore grip, while flat wide-open V sections lend themselves to a scanty fore foot. Bearing this in mind, end sections should be chosen to suit the waters and sailing in view, on the principle that wide-open V sections are fast, especially in light displacement hulls, but slam or produce an uncomfortable jerky motion in short seas. On smooth water easy motion need not prejudice speed, but for estuary work where tides run strongly, and in fact for all serious cruising at sea, moderate V sections are preferable, so that in the inevitable pitching the ends cut into the waves with a steady retardation of swing.

The exact shape chosen for the sections depends, too, on the amount of overhang adopted. Apart from rule dodging a useful property of overhangs is to steady a boat's motion amongst waves that would cause a plumb-ended hull to pitch violently. All sea-going boats occasionally find a sea that seems particularly bent on stopping their progress. Short-ended boats crash into it flinging water aside or taking it aboard, and the wind is shaken out of their sails. That overhangs reduce this motion there is no doubt, for the trouble arises when the distance between successive waves fits the length of the boat. A plumb-ended boat finds a series of such waves an almighty nuisance, but once a boat with overhangs starts pitching, her effective length changes by reason of the overhanging bows and counter whose reserve buoyancy supports the boat's ends so that the sea is no longer the menace it was. Pitching starts, but is kept within reasonable limits.

The flow of water under the tuck, or after part of the run, shoots up behind a transom sterned boat and makes a wave that is caught up and sucked along by

39

the immersed part of the transom, forming eddies as it does so. This can be seen in any square-ended boat, dinghy or cruiser. By carrying on the run well clear of the water-level the attendant drag is eliminated, but one then has a counter stern of one form or another.

A counter can be a good form of stern, both elegant and useful, but it can be a danger to a sea-going boat if run out to a long slender point ; such an end is constructionally weak and lacks buoyancy at the end just where it is needed. The most efficient is the short cut-off counter, a form which offends some tastes in lines. A short canoe stern is a compromise and considered by some to be the finest form of stern for a sea-going cruiser, but in this matter of stern overhang one may note the practice of fishermen few of whom have developed the sharp stern. Certain Cornish luggers are fine examples of it, but it has been stated that these boats were built with sharp sterns only because it eased the handling of their particular nets.[1] Were any form of stern vitally better than another, it would probably have become universal and nets handled accordingly rather than the evolution of the stern been subjected to the convenience of fishing ; it seems that there is no conclusive evidence that either sharp sterns or counter sterns can be hailed as intrinsically more seaworthy.

At the other end of the ship long overhanging bows call for the same comments. Headsails can be handled without the need for a bowsprit if the stem is run out far enough, but a long snout lacks buoyancy and strength. One may say, in short, that reasonable overhangs are good features if one does not mind paying for them.

[1] Sir Herbert Russell in *The Field*, April 25, 1936.

40

ADDITIONAL NOTES ON HULL FORM

V

SAIL PLAN AND RIG

Latterly fashions in sail plans have been as variable
as weathercocks, and in the next decade some new
development will like as not make the wishbone rig
seem antiquated. The fact is that problems of rig and
sails have ceased to be regarded as matters for a fisher-

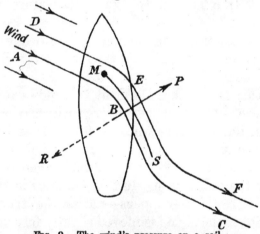

FIG. 9.—The wind's pressure on a sail.

man's counsel and our instructors have become aero-
nautical scientists; and although some dispute any
consequent improvement, there is no doubt that high-
brow investigations have revealed strange happenings
round and about a ship's sails.

Referring to fig. 9, the line MS represents the sail.

The wind blowing from the port side divides to windward of the mast and follows two paths, one ABC which strikes the windward side of the sail and another DEF which passes to leeward of the sail and joins up again with the general wind direction astern of the ship. It is clear that the wind along ABC will push the sails in the direction P, but the experts have found that the wind along DEF sucks the sail in the direction P and that this suction on the leeward side is greater than the push on the windward side.

Then again they prove that the half of the sail near the leading edge M is far more effective than the half near the trailing edge S. And again, that a curved sail is better than a flat sail, though the curvature must not be too great.

But in spite of all this theoretical knowledge the part of practical importance is still the force P at right angles to the general line of the sail MS.

How this force takes the boat to windward has oft-times been explained generally with maths testing diagrams, but for those whose hobby it is and not profession, the simplest way to understand it is to tie a string to a toy railway truck and pull it gently at right angles to the rails ; in fig. 10 this would be in the direction OQ. Nothing happens—unless the truck turns over. But if the string is moved slightly forward into a direction OP, making an angle less than 90 degrees with the rails, a gentle pull moves the truck along the rails.

The condition for forward movement in a ship corresponds exactly. If the force P of fig. 9 acts at an angle less than 90 degrees with the fore and aft line of the ship, the ship moves forward. Engineers then say the wind's force has a forward component, and this forward component (coming from the wind force P at right angles to the sail MS) moves the ship forward.

The wheel flanges keep the truck on the rails, otherwise the truck would move in the direction of the string, and in the same way the lateral area of the hull immersed

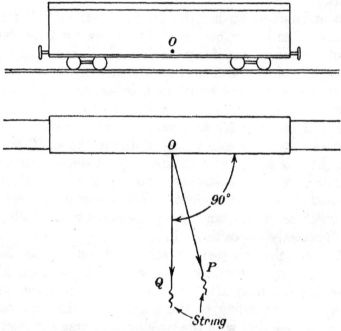

FIG. 10.—Analogy of sailing to windward.

in the water keeps a boat from moving sideways. Unfortunately, though, this broadside pressure is not as effective as the railway lines and a certain amount of leeway does take place.

Another complication to the sailing man arises because the strength of force P in fig. 9 depends on the angle between the sail plan and the wind, i.e. between MS and AB. If we try and point a ship almost into the wind the sails remain just full, but the driving force P will fall away to so small an amount that the ship scarcely moves. It is in trimming the sails and setting a course to best advantage that a skilled sailorman excels.

To understand further the theory of sailing and the balance of sail plan one must know the fundamental law of mechanics that if any moving thing is maintaining a straight course at constant speed, then any forces that are acting on it must annul each other, or cancel out. If forces do not cancel each other the thing they act upon will move faster or slower or turn about.

Now in fig. 9 there is a force P due to the wind, and if the boat is sailing at a constant speed there must be another force equal in strength and opposite in direction to cancel the effect of the first. Such a force comes from the water resistance, and is represented by the dotted line R exactly opposite to P.

At first sight this seems a strange direction, for the boat is moving forwards and the water resistance would naturally be a drag aft. It is the boat's resistance to leeway (corresponding to the pressure of the rails on the truck) together with the resistance or drag opposing forward motion that gives a combined effect called a resultant force, in the direction R. So long as R is equal in strength and opposite in direction to P the boat sails steadily ; but force R can differ from P either by being equal but not opposite, or by being opposite but not equal, or again by being neither equal nor opposite to P. If R is opposite to but less in strength than P the boat gathers way until the water resistance equals the wind's driving force and R equals P. In fig. 11

P and R are equal in strength but not opposite. There is a distance *ab* between their lines of action, and clearly their effect is to turn the boat round.

It happens sometimes that the distance *ab* is small, and then a boat will turn slightly until the effect of wind and water is such as to bring the forces P and R into line. An instance of this is a well-behaved model

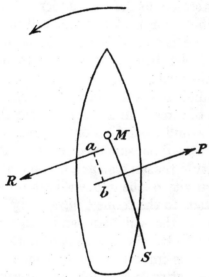

FIG. 11.—Forces of wind and water.

yacht; if the wind veers or backs slightly the model turns one way or another until the wind strikes the sails from the same relative direction.

If, however, *ab* is large, the forces never come into line as the boat turns, and she would go on turning for ever but for coming head to wind or getting into a position with jib aback. When sailing a steady course, if the rudder is put across one way or another the effect may be regarded as changing the line of action of the force R, so upsetting the steady sailing condition of the boat; according to the direction of the rudder so R moves either forward or aft and the boat turns accordingly.

When sailing a straight course at constant speed forces P and R are equal and opposite, but to get the best out of a boat this state of equality must not be obtained by excessive use of the rudder. If a boat will only sail with her helm hard over the sail plan does not suit the hull, and is sometimes said to be unbalanced. Moving the sail plan bodily forward or aft may effect a cure in an unbalanced boat.

A practical difficulty arises in that no one knows the exact position of force P in a sail plan, nor the position of force R in a hull design. For the purpose of comparison, however, P is supposed to act through the centre of gravity of the sail plan as a whole, and R through the centre of gravity of the immersed lateral area of the hull; which leads to the terms *Centre of Effort* (or C.E.) for the centre of the sail plan, and *Centre of Lateral Resistance* (or C.L.R.) for the centre of the immersed lateral area. It is important to remember that these points are only datum points for comparison of yachts and not in fact what their names would imply.

It is certain that the positions of P and R are really well in front of the centres of gravity of sail plan and lateral area, and it is a matter of experience that for good balance between sail plan and hull the centre of effort of the sail plan should be in front of the centre of lateral resistance of the hull. By how much the C.E. should lead the C.L.R. depends on the shape of the sails and hull, and it is usually between 5 per cent and 15 per cent of the water-line length.

For a new design it is wise to find a well-balanced ship of roughly similar proportions, and arrange for the new boat's C.E. to lead her C.L.R. by about the same amount. Only experience enables a designer to get it right, and then, not infrequently, only after a bad first shot.

Sail area naturally means speed, for sails provide the driving force, and thinking only of speed on a perfect day one would set the largest sails the ship could carry, with spars to suit. But seaworthiness demands moderation, and whether the limit is set by experience or by rule it is really due to respect for the might of wind and water.

The designer's problem in these days is to get the greatest driving force from a restricted sail plan ; and his choice of rig like his choice of hull form is going to be the most efficient that the intended use permits, which has led to the big problems of rig—whether to adopt one large mainsail or two smaller ones, cutter, yawl, or ketch in fact ; and whether to have bermuda or gaff mainsails.

The old-fashioned lug sail is, for fishing boats or tenders, a simple rig which enables a useful sail area to be set on relatively short spars. A mast whose length above the gunwales is no more than the dinghy's overall length can very well be made stout enough to stand without shrouds ; and such a mast stepped well forward rigged with a standing lug means only one halliard to the mast-head, a halliard that can be arranged as forestay by leading it through a block on the stem to a cleat aft.

Almost the antithesis of this is the 14-foot international. The height of the mast is limited by rule or

D   49

it would not stop where it does at 22½ feet above the gunwale, and although the bermuda rig is not compulsory it is naturally used for racing. A gunter lug is a compromise, since the mast is shorter for a sail area not much less efficient than the bermudian, and possessing heavy weather advantages.

Many small boat owners swear by a roller jib, but this entails a round wooden roller in the luff of the sail which causes eddies in its wake. A neat way of surmounting this drawback is to double the luff of the jib, so forming a pocket into which the roller is slipped loosely ; the sail pulls out evenly on either side, see

FIG. 12.—Double luff on roller jib.

fig. 12, with the result that the roller presents a round leading edge to the wind while gradually tapering to the sail proper, all of which is according to the best aerodynamic theory. To make the sail roll up without slipping it is tied tightly to the roller at frequent intervals ; the lashing for this is rove through eyelet-holes in the jib arranged carefully to come at either side of the roller so that the tapering shape of the pocket is retained.

This form is often called a double luff and suitably modified has been applied to mainsails with a view to reducing the wind resistance of the mast.

The choice of bermudian or gaff rig is really a choice between a more effective sail area and one of proved reliability in emergency. Modern work has proved the effectiveness of tall narrow sails and the value of long luffs for windward work, and in modern bermudian mainsails the ratio of luff to foot, called the aspect ratio, varies from two upwards to about three and a half, when the sail becomes too tall to set properly. A comparison of the proportions in general use for the two types of rig is shown in fig. 13. One sometimes finds bermuda-rigged cruisers with an aspect ratio barely exceeding one and a half, a shape which has lost the effectiveness of the rig though retaining the other advantage of the bermudian mainsail, a single halliard.

The mechanical difficulties of the bermudian rig have nearly all been successfully overcome, but for good results it is essential to use modern tracks and give them regular attention. Failure of any part of the rigging may lead to such serious consequences that neither bermudian nor gaff rigs can be regarded as fool-proof.

In small craft for cruising or racing the sloop rig is the simplest and most effective for a given sail area (the sloop rig is that with a single foresail). A small bermudian sloop with roller reefing foresail and mainsail is as easily handled as anything one can find, but in boats over 20 feet on the water line the foresail is usually too big to roll up properly in any weight of wind. Seventy square feet is big enough for a roller reefing headsail, and larger sloops use an ordinary staysail hanked to the forestay. Cruising yachts are frequently short-handed, clumsily handled, or even single-handed, and convenience is a very reasonable prior claim to speed. For such two small headsails are better than

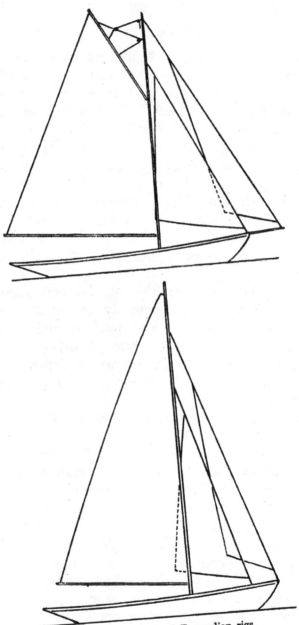

FIG. 13.—Gaff and Bermudian rigs.

one, for either or both can be fitted with roller reefing or Wykeham Martin gear (the latter, though not a reefing gear, enables the crew to roll up one headsail completely without leaving the cockpit).

One roller gear is enough if fitted to the right sail. On older ships with straight stems and long bowsprits the staysail was the first to come off, and one often sees the roller here ; but the modern yacht with well-rounded or cut-away stem and bermuda mainsail should balance easily under her reefed mainsail and staysail so that the less accessible jib should have the roller gear.

The fore triangle is so often out of sight that it is often out of mind ; attention to jib and staysail will do wonders to the performance of many ships. The present tendency is towards a sail plan all inboard, and a very short bowsprit has been proved adequate even in cruising cutters. The staysail is hanked to a forestay leading through the deck well abaft the stem head, and a short boom with efficient bermudian mainsail matched by a tall narrow jib.

The jib can set up an enormous pull on the mast, and as the longer the luff the greater the pull, the jib should not reach the mast-head unless it is intended to hand the jib as soon as the wind shows signs of piping up. Such a scheme has proved successful in ocean racing with a modern fast hull.

Headsail sheet leads are often in the wrong place. The sheet should come away from the jib or staysail so that on a wind if the sheet is gradually eased off the whole luff lifts and starts shaking at the same time. Very often the upper part of the sail starts first and as the sheet is eased off further the shaking spreads, which of course may be the fault of the sail but is more often due to the sheet lead being too far aft. The best position for this depends on the shape of the sail and is most satisfactorily found by trial.

The total sail area a ship can carry with advantage depends on her form, a heavy beamy ship standing up to a lot of canvas better than a light displacement hull; but the area is largely determined by the height of the mast, a height settled by the designer's decision regarding seaworthiness and adequate sail area. In a bermudian cutter a mast height about 1·7 times the length of the water line is found to be a good proportion, but there is no rigid rule.

While considering sail plans it is well to note that for many small cruisers with beamy comfort below decks the bermudian rig offers no advantage over the gaff, for the great feature of the bermudian rig is pointing up well to windward and beamy boats generally need sailing rather free and fast. Off the wind the gaff rig shines, and experience seems to prove that it is the better rig for certain boats.

The position of a cutter's mast in relation to her water line varies considerably in different yachts. The fisherman's rule was to put the mast of a cutter at two-fifths of the L.W.L. from the fore end, an excellent rule for modern boats as well, as it brings the windage of the rigging reasonably far aft, so preventing the ship's head blowing off excessively when under much-reduced sail or when hove to, and it helps to keep the mainsail a manageable size.

Two-fifths of the water line, however, generally brings the mast into the cabin, and some people object either to the mast being in the cabin or to the small cabin-top necessary if the mast is to go through the deck in front of it. So the mast goes right forward and the mainsail with it.

With a nice sailing breeze and whole sail set this is a grand place for the mast ; it is when reefed that the trouble begins. As the bermudian sail is reefed the C.E. moves forward, as can be seen at once by sketching the two triangles, whole sail and reefed, and noting the positions of the two C.E.s. Compensation can be made by taking in headsails, but only to a limited extent, and with a mast too far forward a bermuda rigged ship may be hard headed under whole sail and yet carry lee helm when reefed right down.

For sea-going ships it is wise to keep the mast weight inboard and its windage as far aft as possible; but if accommodation insists on a mast well forward, or if the rather greater adaptability of a two-masted rig is desired, one can move the mast forward with its top cut off and set up astern as a mizen—yawl, ketch, or schooner, according to the size of the mizen, which in a schooner has become the largest sail and is called the mainsail. Seldom if ever does one find a schooner under 12 tons, and a designer debarred from the cutter rig has a choice of yawl or ketch.

Opinions differ as to the efficiency of a yawl. Certain racing rules do not count the area of the mizen, so that naturally enough it features in yachts designed for races under this rule, although it has been generally agreed that a yawl's mizen is of little use to windward. A staysail set on a temporary mizen forestay has become a popular reaching sail of late.

Staying the mast is an acute problem in these days of light hollow spars. Shrouds, forestays, backstays, and spreaders are all of vital importance. The old idea

55

of a mast was a stout spar holding up the rigging with a little support from shrouds; but now it is regarded only as a strut, one member of a complicated system of rigging members each of which is scientifically proportioned to do its bit in withstanding wind forces. It must be confessed, however, that designers are as yet not very good at doing this, and that most masts are still doing quite a lot of the stout spar business.

Whatever form is adopted the forward pull of the forestay and jib should be countered by some form of stay leading aft, either by ordinary runners or by some more modern system of standing backstay and jumper struts. In considering the forces on the mast and standing rigging one should remember that the mainsail applies a distributed force along the length of the mast from gooseneck to peak, and in addition transmits the pull of the mainsheet to the mast, all of which vary in intensity and direction according to the strength of the wind and the point of sailing; meanwhile as the luff of a bermudian sail does not come away radially from the mast it applies a torque or twist as well as a direct pull.

A rough rule for the size of the shrouds is that all together they should be able to support twice the weight of the hull; but never forget that rigging screws, chainplates, and rivets, etc., must all stand up to the pull in the attached shroud.

ADDITIONAL NOTES ON RIGGING AND SAILS

VI

CONSTRUCTION

The designer's work does not end with completion of lines, accommodation and sail plans. The shipbuilding part of the work, the actual construction, is at least equally important. As few plans become real ships as dream ships become real plans ; but if a ship is really passing beyond dreams and paper it is worth ensuring that the last important metamorphosis is to the satisfaction of the designer.

To the owner who undertakes the actual building himself the workmanship is as good as he can do, and for any faults only himself is to blame ; but few of us have time to build anything larger than a dinghy, which is all to the good of the professional builder though worrying to the designer. A good man can be trusted to make a good job of a boat, given the lines and accommodation and sail plans, and he can often improve the details from his experience ; but unless you know his reputation as a builder is unimpeachable it is as well to tell him how and of what you want the boat built. Remember, a number of builders never sail themselves.

General constructional features are shown in fig. 14, the names of the various parts being given therein. In some districts local names exist, but these are in general use. The word shelf seems to be used indis-

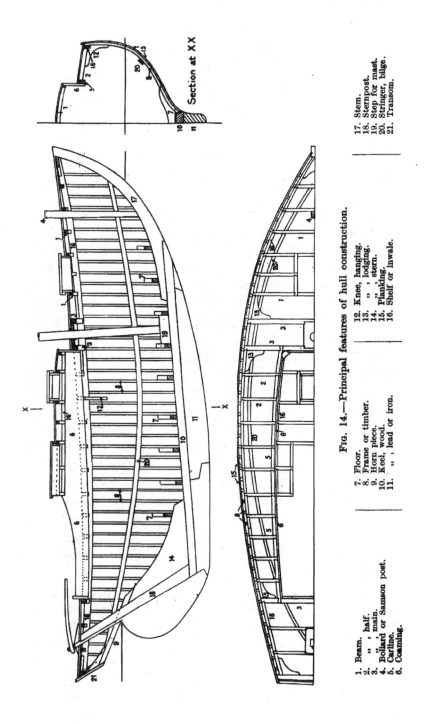

Fig. 14.—Principal features of hull construction.

1. Beam.
2. " , half.
3. " , main.
4. Bollard or Samson post.
5. Carline.
6. Coaming.

7. Floor.
8. Frame or timber.
9. Horn piece.
10. Keel, wood.
11. " , lead or iron.

12. Knee, hanging.
13. " , lodging.
14. " , stern.
15. Planking.
16. Shelf or inwale.

17. Stem.
18. Sternpost.
19. Step for mast.
20. Stringer, bilge.
21. Transom.

Section at X X

criminately, and although one presumes this applies when that stout piece of timber carries deck beams, the word inwale would be a more accurate generalization. The gunwale was a wale to take the gundeck of old men-of-war.

To a certain extent planking and deck may be regarded as a skin put on to a strong hull framework of keel, frames, beams, etc. ; and to get the necessary strength without unnecessary wood is part of the designer's job ; also, more often than not, to know what methods and materials to specify for a combination of cheapness and sound construction.

Building procedure is more or less as follows. From the plans and specifications and table of offsets a full-size drawing is made of the half sections, the stem, the sternpost, and generally of the whole lines of the ship. Full-size templates or patterns of the complete sections called the moulds, are cut from wood, and also patterns of the stem, sternpost and knee. From the latter patterns the actual part is marked on a suitable piece of timber, and cut out, and then these parts are bolted to the keel. If there is a counter the horn piece is joined on now.

Then the transom is cut out and fixed directly to the sternpost, or if there is a counter, to the hornpiece by a knee. The rabbet for the planking is cut—the rabbet is a groove in the keel, stem and sternpost to take the edges of the planks joining on to them (see fig. 15)—and the notches to take the lower ends of the frames.

At this condition the keel is drilled for the many bolts that pass through it, and the iron or lead ballast keel is bolted on, although in small boats this is sometimes left until later. Lead ballast seldom extends as

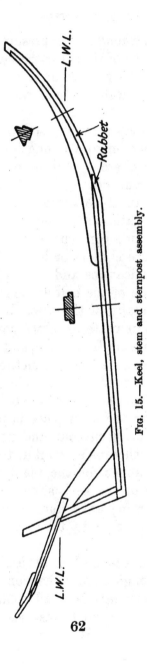

Fig. 15.—Keel, stem and sternpost assembly.

62

far as the sternpost and there is in consequence a gap
abaft the lead, which gap is filled with a false keel of
timber, sometimes known as a barn piece. Lead being
none too strong should not be run out to a point at
the forward end, but cut off while still fairly thick and
the tapering gap filled with timber.

The keel, stem and sternpost are now set up at their
proper angle to the water line (see fig. 15), and the
moulds fixed to it vertically in their proper positions.
Ribbands follow ; these are substantial battens nailed
over the moulds as though they were planks, well spaced,
however, and temporarily secured to stem, moulds, sternpost and transom. These ribbands give the shape of the
hull, and the timbers or frames are fitted inside them,
so taking up their proper shape for the finished hull.

Planking then begins, and as this proceeds, the ribbands come off one by one to make way for the planks
which are fastened to the frames. After the planking
is finished the moulds are done with and come out,
and the shelf and bilge stringers can go in. With the
moulds removed only the shell of the hull is left, and
to prevent it opening out sideways a few clamps are
fitted across the topmost planks.

Floors can go in now, secured to bolts ready for them
in the keel.

The main beams are fitted and those going from shelf
to shelf, then the carlines, half beams, lodging and
hanging knees, mast partners, and rudder trunk or tube
all in order. Also the coamings and cabin-top beams.
The inside bulkheads are more easily fitted at this stage
before the deck goes on, particularly in small boats.
The deck with the hatches and skylights completes
the hull.

This is the builder's part. The designer is concerned with each part in detail. Materials and scantlings are his affair, and these vary according to the intended use of the ship and the ideas of the designer. Lloyd's have produced a book of rules for the construction of yachts, and although many long-lived ships have lighter work in them, these rules set the standard for first-class construction.

The form of the ship as well as her tonnage determines the scantlings to be used, and one must consult the book itself for any particular application ; but scantlings which would be approved for our example ship of fig. 3 are set out on page 65, and give an idea of the standard demanded. Dimensions are not everything, however, and to be classed at Lloyd's both quality and workmanship have to satisfy the surveyor. " Rules for the construction and classification of wood yachts " can be obtained by courtesy of Lloyd's Register Committee, 71 Fenchurch Street, London E.C.3, price 21s.

Keel. English Elm and Oak are mostly used. Oak is good in dinghies and small craft, but where a considerable width of timber is involved its habit of marked shrinking on drying out and opening up again on soaking sets up enormous stresses in adjoining members. Elm is not so bad in this respect, and has the great advantage that it is generally reliable and can be obtained in large widths. Elm is liable to rot in fresh water and in positions between wind and water where it alternately soaks and dries.

In the days of straight stems keels were generally parallel to the water line, but now that a cut-away or rounded fore foot is almost invariable keels are

SCANTLINGS FOR 6-TON CRUISER

Part	Moulding	Siding	Remarks
Keel	$3\frac{1}{2}''$	$7\frac{1}{2}''$	
Stem and Sternpost	$3\frac{1}{2}''$	$3\frac{1}{2}''$	siding increased towards scarph to fit keel
Frames, bent only	$1\frac{5}{8}''$	$1\frac{1}{2}''$	spaced $6\frac{1}{2}''$ centres
Frames, grown only (at heel)	$2\frac{3}{8}''$	$1\frac{7}{8}''$	spaced $12\frac{1}{2}''$ centres
Floors, G.I. (at throat) for bent frames only	$\frac{5}{8}''$	$1\frac{1}{8}''$	} for oak floors increase sectional area seven times
Floors, G.I. (at throat) for grown frames only	$\frac{5}{8}''$	$1\frac{5}{8}''$	
Main Beams	$3\frac{1}{2}''$	$2\frac{1}{4}''$	spaced $12\frac{1}{2}''$ normally
Ordinary Beams	$2''$	$1\frac{1}{16}''$	spaced $12''$ normally
Shelf	Area to be 7 square inches		
Bilge Stringer	Area to be $5\frac{1}{2}$ square inches		
Planking and Deck	$\frac{7}{8}''$ thick		

65

inclined ; setting the keel up at a good angle while one is about it, has the advantage that it drains bilge water aft quickly, where the pump can pretty well dry out the ship.

Ballast. Reasonable choice is between cast iron and lead, for brass and platinum are beyond normal pockets. Prices vary, but recently, while iron castings were about £8 a ton, lead castings at their lowest were some £20 a ton and have since nearly doubled in cost, hence the frequent use of cast iron in place of lead, an unfortunate circumstance since with modern hulls iron is seldom heavy enough to get the ship down to her marks without the use of inside ballast. On the use of inside ballast opinions are divided, but it certainly means a loss of stiffness and should not feature in racing craft except for trimming ; and in small sea-going ships safety demands sail carrying power which in turn demands stiffness, none of which should be sacrificed if one can help it. When inside ballast has to be shifted it is a trouble, and aboard it tends to induce a dirty bilge smell, and takes up space that may occasionally be very useful in keeping bilge water below the cabin floorboards.

The cost of lead is less than the finished casting, and many builders can cast it themselves, so reducing the cost difference between lead and iron. Lead should be secured by copper, naval brass, or Tungum alloy bolts to minimize galvanic action which in time corrodes one metal or another ; and a thin packing piece of timber between lead and keel proper is a wise means of insulating the lead from the lower ends of bolts securing the floors.

Iron ballast keels should be secured by galvanized-iron keel bolts, well greased before being inserted to facilitate knocking out for inspection after a few years.

The right amount of ballast depends on how heavily a ship is constructed. Uffa Fox shows that in well-built cruisers it is about 45 per cent of the displacement, but it is interesting to note fishing-boat proportions. A Mount's Bay lugger of 10 tons displacement used to carry 7 tons of ballast, but it was inside ballast and the boats themselves were built to carry.

The usual difficulty is to get the weight of a yacht's keel far enough forward. Engines and crew are a very appreciable load in a small ship and bring the stern down, and usually there is space aft beneath the floor-boards for inside trimming ballast, so that in general the centre of gravity of the outside ballast should come a little forward of the ship's centre of buoyancy. With a sloping keel and limited draft space for outside ballast is at a premium, and lead, being nearly 60 per cent heavier than iron, has obvious advantages. When, however, the design happens to give plenty of room for an outside ballast keel, there is no intrinsic advantage of lead over cast iron.

Stem and Sternpost. Oak is general for these, and a piece should be selected with the grain following the curve of the stem. If it cannot be found in one piece, two pieces can be scarphed together (a long overlapping joint), which is better than one piece with a cross-grain.

The sternpost is sometimes halved into the keel, sometimes tenoned into it, and sometimes just bolted on ; this last is not good but seems to hang together satisfactorily if supported by a good stern knee. In

67

small craft this can be one large oak crook, and in larger craft a suitable group of timber deadwoods let into the keel and well fastened together with bolts. If the hull scantlings are light, it is a good thing to let the stern knee overlap considerably the after end of the outside ballast, for the keel of a lightly built ship may bend at this point when she is being handled ashore. It is very easy to arrange, although in first-class work it is unnecessary, as the rest of the hull acts as a girder and no sign of bending would occur.

With a counter the upper part of the sternpost is either continued to the deck and fastened to a beam or carline, or else it is cut off above the hornpiece joint.

Hornpiece. Oak again is used for this. The hornpiece is secured to the sternpost by two side-pieces, the horns, sometimes let into the sternpost. Counters get very hard treatment in bad weather and their strength is important, but the scantlings naturally depend on the size and shape of the counter in relation to the rest of the hull.

Transom. Mahogany is probably the best wood for a transom, as it holds nails well even when driven into it along the grain. It is well to fit fashion pieces, however, and particularly so with other timbers. Fashion pieces are a sort of frame cut to fit into the corner formed by the transom and planking and fastened into it with the grain running along the transom edge ; the planks are then secured by nails driven into the fashion pieces across the grain of the wood.

Timbers or Frames. Grown frames are almost always

of Oak, although Teak and Mahogany are to be found. Grown frames are cut to shape, like the stem, from a solid piece of timber whose grain follows the required curve. Oak, American Rock Elm, and sometimes Ash are used for bent frames, which are steamed and while hot are bent to the proper shape. On steaming, Rock Elm bends without shelling, which sometimes happens to Oak, but there is little to choose between the two. Grown frames are stronger than bent if there is no cross-grain in the wood, and such frames are spaced about twice as far apart as bent frames. The two forms, grown and bent, are frequently used together, say two bent frames between grown frames, and the spacing is arranged accordingly.

All frames should be let into the keel or stem where they abut, unless the hull is very flat, when they can run right across the keel. Forged steel angles are commonly used in place of grown oak frames, but these are beyond the scope of the ordinary builder, who has to cut out a pattern for each steel frame and give it to a smithy skilled in the work.

Floors. These go across the keel and hold the two sides of the boat together. One sometimes finds ships years old held together by their garboard planks only, but it is not a good precedent. Modern construction with outside ballast stresses these parts far more than inside ballast, and floors are a vital part of the construction.

Oak is the usual timber for floors, chosen with the grain of the wood following the curve of the floor. The arms should extend well up the sides of the ship, and the central part be well bolted to the keel. Some

69

builders fit floors at 2 or 3 feet intervals along the keel for half the ship's length only, but for hard use and long life they should be fitted unsparingly, noting that Lloyd's rules call for floors to be fitted on every frame amidships. Galvanized-iron floors are common and have the advantage of taking less space than wood floors, but they have to be forged from templates made for each floor by the builder; these floors may be of flat strip or built up from steel plate.

If the outside ballast keel is of cast iron, keel bolts for wood floors should be of galvanized iron, but if the keel is lead they should be of copper or naval brass; and these bolts should not touch the lead at their lower ends. Iron floors are frequently secured with copper or brass bolts well doped with red lead, but galvanized-iron bolts insulated from the lead at their lower ends are tolerable. Tungum alloy, which has practically no galvanic action with either copper, brass, or lead, is a promising new material for keel fastenings; but unfortunately it is more expensive than copper.

Planking. For racing craft where light weight is of particular advantage, Mahogany is frequently used, while for cruising yachts Teak is considered ideal, though Pitch Pine and Columbian Pine are more commonly used, being good for the job and less expensive than Teak. Oak tends to open up on drying and is not to be recommended for topsides, if at all for planking. Columbian Pine needs very careful selection for anything but inside work.

Clincher built work, that is with overlapping planks, is almost entirely confined to dinghies and small classes of dayboats; for anything larger than this carvel laid planking is used, which presents a smooth surface to the sea. Carvel planking starts with the sheer plank and the garboards ; the latter are the planks next the keel, whose lower edges have to be carefully shaped to fit the rabbet in keel and sternpost. Working from the garboards upwards, the lower edge of each plank is shaped to fit the upper edge of the preceding one, but leaving a narrow V-shaped gap between, with planks touching on the inside. After planking the surface is smoothed off and the gaps caulked by driving in cotton rope and then putty. When first in the water the planks swell and drive out the putty, so that a week or two after launching the hull requires rubbing down and another coat of paint.

A varnished teak sheer plank, the topmost plank, sets off the sheer rather well, but there is no real virtue in it.

Scarphs in planks are often necessary but should be arranged so that the scarph in one plank is well separated from the scarph in the next plank. " No planks to be scarphed " one sometimes sees attached as a condition for small craft where the planks can be cut from one piece, but without a scarph there will be pronounced sny or curve in some of the planks at least, and there is good reason for preferring a scarphed joint.

Owing to the greater draft and hard turn in the bilge by the tuck, the planks have to cover more girth at the run than up forward. This means that the lower planks must be much wider astern than for'ard, and a dodge sometimes used to avoid too great a difference is to shape the plank coming at the hard turn to fit the preceding plank for part of its length only, from the bows to a little abaft the midship section, thereafter letting the plank run on with a straight edge.

71

This leaves a long triangular gap which is subsequently filled with a short plank called a steeler; the narrow end of this should be an inch or more wide and fitted into the adjacent plank, where it can be fastened securely to a frame.

If the hull is to conform accurately to the moulds and lines, the practice of pinning planks should be eschewed. If a plank is not accurately shaped to fit the preceding plank, it will not follow the required curve naturally on bending round the frames, but it can be crushed into position by pinning the ends and forcing the rest of the plank on to the frames. It is then fastened, leaving the wood so stressed that it pulls the frames out of shape.

Shelf. Pitch Pine or Oak are general, with Rock Elm common in dinghies. The shelf goes inside the frames and then the projecting ends of the frames are cut off level with the top plank. In dinghies it is sometimes fitted against the top plank, the frames having first been cut off just beneath it, but this is not such a strong job.

The forward end of the shelf should be fitted into the stem and the two shelves tied together by a stout knee or breast hook. Sometimes this is omitted without incurring disaster, but it is none the less to be advised. Lloyd's rules insist on the shelf being through fastened at every frame, but many experienced builders fasten at alternate frames only. The after ends are tied to the transom by knees.

Bilge Stringers. Pitch Pine is usual unless one can pay for Teak. Like the shelf, stringers should be fastened at every frame to meet Lloyd's approval, although

this is not the practice in many experienced yards ; and
the ends should be tied together by knees in counsel of
perfection. Bilge stringers are often omitted in craft
under 3 tons, or run for the middle half of the ship
only. Do not put them in the drawing where they will
be in the way of the saloon seats, ready to give one a
dig in the bony part of the back ; an inch or so up or
down makes a lot of difference to comfort.

Beams. Oak is the best timber for beams. These
run athwartships and are dovetailed into the shelf on
either side. Beams in way of the mast should be amply
strong enough as they are the longest in the ship and
get most of the work ; those beams at the ends of deck
openings, such as cabins and cockpits, should also be
stouter than the others as they have the carlines let
into them.

Beams are arched slightly to give a cambered deck,
the amount of camber depending on the size of ship
and the designer's fancy. For small craft it may be
as much as $\frac{1}{2}$ inch per foot of beam, but in large ships
$\frac{1}{4}$ inch is more usual ; whatever it is, the same curvature
is usually maintained throughout the ship. Cabin-top
beams are cambered to taste, often with a great rise
amidships for the sake of the headroom it gives.

Some builders think a joint is perfect if it is dovetailed, whereas in fact joints need a little common sense
besides. Beams should be dovetailed into the shelf so
that the weight of the deck tends to drive them in ; and
carlines should be dovetailed likewise into the beams at
either end.

Spacing of the beams depends on their position in the
ship, for it is usual to secure bulkheads to beams and

frames; and in thinking out the design one has to arrange for the principal bulkheads to come where a beam can conveniently be lined up with one of the frames. This fixes the position of one or two beams and the rest are spaced out evenly between them. For good work one beam to every two bent frames, where bent frames only are fitted, is a rough guide; but there is one old fishing boat some 24 feet over all built with 2½-inch by 2-inch beams spaced nearly 30 inches which to my knowledge has seen her three score years and ten, so one cannot lay down the law about closely spaced beams. The thickness of the deck has a good deal to do with it, too, and in this boat the deck is far thicker than is usual in yachts to-day.

Carlines. These are of Oak or Pitch Pine. Alongside the big opening in the deck for cabin and cockpit they take the half beams under the side decks and are generally rather more in depth than the beams. To hold them to their proper curvature they are tied to the shelf by two or three copper bolts. At hatches and skylights it is common practice to dispense with carlines proper and secure the coamings of hatch or skylight to the beams and deck beneath, cutting away any deck and beams that would occupy the opening; the cut ends of such beams are supported by a through fastening to the coaming above, and although it may not seem the neatest finish, long practice with hefty coamings establishes its adequate strength.

Cabin-top beams are sometimes dovetailed directly into the coamings, but if so, beware of leaks from above. It is better to let the cabin-top beams into a small shelf or inwale secured along the top of the coamings on the

74

inside, but if this practice is not followed the beam-ends which pass through the coamings must be carefully packed with white lead and the edges covered with beading.

Knees. Grown Oak crooks or forged iron galvanized are used for these. Lodging knees are those between the beams and the shelf, hanging knees are those between the beams and the topsides or frames. Mast and rigging are fairly concentrated, but the weight of hull and keel together with the righting moment of the hull itself are distributed along the length of the hull, and when heeled this tends to make the planks slide edgewise, plank along plank, and the beams to set at an angle athwartships. In some modern work the hull is cross-braced to preserve its rigidity, but generally it is the lodging knees that are particularly important in meeting the stresses set up on heeling.

Decks. Teak is the best wood for decks, and because decks are so conspicuous it is frequently used in spite of its cost. Yellow Pine is a good alternative which gives clean white decks, but real yellow pine is scarce. Deck planks may be straight with their ends worked into the covering board, the outermost deck plank which is shaped to follow the curvature of the topside plank and shelf ; or the deck planks may be curved following the shape of the covering board and let into a king plank, a straight wide plank running fore and aft along the midship line. A teak deck in a seven-tonner may well cost £20 for timber alone, so that the humbler alternative of a canvas-covered pine deck is naturally popular. If painted with an anti-skid paint, it has great advantages, and there are quite a number of teak laid decks covered with canvas and painted, not to keep them watertight but because their owners have the courage to prefer a secure foothold at sea to a smart appearance at moorings.

The planking under the canvas must be really dry when it is put on. Unseasoned wood will shrink when hot with heat-wave sunshine and leave a gap bridged by canvas ; and then in damp weather the gap closes again and pushes up the canvas into a little ridge ; soon the canvas splits and the decks leak badly. The decks themselves should be well painted before the canvas goes on.

Rudders. Oak or Elm is usual for rudder-blades. The rudder stock or head joining the rudder to the tiller is either a stout piece of timber or a metal rod. For a transom sterned ship a timber head is very satisfactory, but where the ship has a counter the rudder head passes through a trunk, supposedly watertight, and here the large size of a timber head is a disadvantage ; a metal rod working in a metal tube can more readily be made watertight. Wood heads are common, however, and on account of their greater diameter work in wooden trunks built up through the counter. It is these wooden trunks that so often leak in old boats.

ADDITIONAL NOTES ON CONSTRUCTION

PART II

THE PRACTICE OF DESIGN

VII

DRAWING

The Lines.

To put on paper the lines of a yacht hitherto but dreamed of, takes longer than looking at other folks' drawings, but is no more difficult than understanding them.

With something of the sort in mind, the lines of fig. 16 come into existence by a process as follows. The load water-line LW is first drawn, LW being the proposed water-line length to a convenient scale, say 1 inch to a foot, and then the mid-point on LW is put in at M. Vertical lines are then drawn through L, M, and W and continued downwards to *l*, *m*, and *w*, on the centre-line of the half-breadth plan. Continuing LW to the right and marking on it the two points P and Q just to define this line, another line YOZ is drawn at right angles to PQ.

The profile of the ship is then sketched in freehand, SFJWRTULS; likewise the half-breadth deck line S*defghj*. Here one is giving the first definite form on paper to one's ideas. A mental picture of the ship, and the general proportions of beam and draft discussed in Chapter IV of Part I, suffice at this stage to give an outline, though it may be expedient to amend it later as the drawing proceeds point by point towards completion.

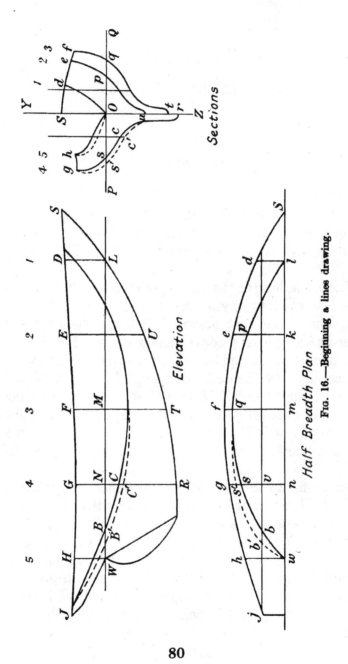

FIG. 16.—Beginning a lines drawing.

So fig. 16 commences. Obviously the deck amidships must be as wide on the half-breadth plan as on the sections drawing, which means that from f to YZ on the sections drawing equals mf on the half-breadth plan; also f to OQ equals FM. We also have that Ot on the sections drawing equals MT on the elevation drawing. Thus the points f and t on the sections drawing are fixed as soon as the profile and half deck line are drawn. After putting these points in the section drawing the half section fqt can be drawn, as pleasing a shape as possible provided only that it passes through f and t. Only a half section is drawn, for both sides of the ship are alike.

There is nothing more difficult than this in all the drawing except that to get neat smooth curves freehand drawing has to be abandoned when a few more points get settled.

Having reached the stage described, the load water line on the half-breadth plan goes in. Before drawing it in the point q on the half-breadth plan can be marked, for Oq on the section already drawn equals mq on the half breadth. The L.W.L. starts at l, passes through q and finishes at w; the intermediate parts are drawn in by eye to a shape we hope will turn out well later.

In the sections drawing the two points d and O are now fixed for number 1 section; on number 2 section the three points e, p, and u; on number 4 section the three points g, s and r; and on number 5 section the two points h and O. These sections are now drawn in through these points as shown by the full lines.

Once these five sections are drawn the buttock line on the elevation has five points settled for it, of which C is an example—for NC on the elevation equals the distance from c to PQ on number 4 section. The buttock line also has three points given by the water line and deck line of the half-breadth plan, of which B is an example—for NB on the elevation equals vb on the half breadth.

Perhaps the buttock line drawn through these points does not seem a fair smooth curve, or perhaps number 4 section is not full enough to please ; it is in deciding these things that experience counts. Anyhow, not being satisfied with number 4 section as drawn, we sketch in the dotted one. At once the other drawings need attention. On the elevation the buttock line must pass through C', and this makes it cut the water line at B' instead of B. The water-line on the half-breadth plan must now go through s' instead of s and through b' instead of b, s' being fixed by the dotted section and b' by the amended buttock, for ns' on the half breadth equals Os' on the sections, and vb' on the half breadth equals NB' on the elevation.

As the number of curves increases, kinks may occur and smoothing out the lines involves adjusting all the other lines affected, a tedious job called fairing up.

The lines so far described are all contours of vertical or horizontal slices. Diagonals are made by slanting slices. In fig. 3 there are two diagonals which on the sections appear as straight lines sloping away from the central axis, and each of these gives the angle of a slice extending from stem to stern. With complete sections instead of half sections these sloping lines would be necessary only on one side of the axis. As it is, some sections are on one side of the axis and some on the other side, and the diagonals must be put in on both sides of the vertical axis ; but each pair meeting on the axis represents only one slice. In drawing these diagonals great care must be taken to make the angle with the axis exactly the same on both sides.

The distance measured along one of these diagonal lines from the axis to each section is marked off on the half-breadth plan giving a series of points like those of the water lines, and the curve through these is drawn in ; to distinguish these diagonal curves from the water lines they would be drawn below the line *lw* of fig. 16.

Another important curve is the actual shape of the transom, which the builder will want to know. In fig. 3 the transom appears on the sections drawing, but while the half breadths shown there are correct, the heights shown are only the vertical heights above the L.W.L. The real shape is shown on the left of the elevation drawing. This shape is found by projecting lines at right angles to the sloping transom, such as those marked dotted, and then marking off on these projected lines the half breadths of the transom found on the sections drawing for the water lines whose ends start the dotted lines.

It is the builder's job to turn the lines into a boat, which he does by building the hull round wooden moulds which are full-size copies of the complete sections, set up along the keel in positions given by the elevation drawing. Builders, however, are seldom expert with ruler and dividers and if a designer wants a boat anything like his design it behoves him to make the builder's job as easy as possible.

The first move on the builder's part is to make a full-size copy of the sections, chalked or pencilled somewhere on a level floor. To facilitate this a table of offsets should be given him. This table gives enough dimensions of the drawing, full size, to enable the sections to be laid off—half breadths and spacing of sections, and the depths from L.W.L. to buttock lines, etc. ; and because it is the outside of the planking that must correspond to the dimensions of the drawing the moulds must be made smaller than the sections by the thickness of the planking. This correction for planking thickness is made in the table of offsets.

It is not necessary to redraw the sections of fig. 3 to get the dimensions corrected for planking thickness. Setting the dividers to the thickness (according to scale) and using this to mark off points on the water lines, diagonals and buttocks inside the original section contours is all that is necessary. This thickness must always be marked off normal to the section contour, not horizontally along the water lines.

Having marked these points on the drawing the lengths are measured off in inches and decimals, and then converted into full-size dimensions. Builders work to an accuracy of about one-quarter of an inch, which is reasonable enough, for on a drawing to a scale of 1 inch to a foot one-fiftieth of an inch represents roughly one-quarter of an inch ; in dinghy drawings to a larger scale this accuracy could, of course, be improved.

The whole boat is faired up again by bending long strips of wood, the ribbands, round the moulds, and if nothing is more than a quarter of an inch out the drawing and laying off are good. A builder with experience of drawings from many sources, including one of the most renowned firms, remarked to me that " amateur's drawings are the most accurate." He was referring particularly to designs by Dr. Harrison Butler, whose drawings must be the envy of all amateur designers.

The Construction Drawing.

Many books have been written about mechanical drawing, but they are all really about conventions and dodges used in drawing various mechanical items ; and all that designers of boats need know is those conventions that affect their pleasure. Here again more can be learnt from the study of examples than from the reading of many words. It will suffice to say that in mechanical drawing one views the subject from three directions at right angles exactly as in fig. 3, elevation, plan, and cross-sections ; and one draws the profiles of all the solid substance one sees without regard to perspective shadows or reflections.

When it is important to show anything that is concealed by something in front of it, it is represented by dotted lines ; but refrain from excessive use of these, as they are often confusing.

In constructional drawings of boats one is generally concerned with the inside of the hull, and this calls for imagination. The hull is treated as though sliced down the fore-and-aft vertical centre line and what one would see of the resulting apparition is then drawn. Similarly cross-sections are drawn, the positions of the cross-sections being chosen to show the actual interior to best advantage. Where the cross-section cuts through a solid piece of wood as keel or deck, the cut part is shaded. The wood graining one often sees is not essential ; it is only the pretty fancy of a skilled draughtsman.

The Rigging and Sail Plans.

Rigging and sail plans are simpler than the lines and present little difficulty from the draughtsman's point of view. The sails themselves are shown flat and stretched out fore and aft. Even square sails are frequently shown thus, but it is better to show these on a separate view looking from stem to stern.

A smaller scale than that used for the lines and construction drawings is generally adequate for a sail plan, but small details such as blocks and purchases cannot be shown on it, and if these are not adequately defined in the specification a separate drawing on a larger scale is necessary. Sometimes such detail drawings can be shown as inserts on the sail plan.

General Comments.

In constructional drawings write in all the important dimensions. The builder will do his best, but his dividers are probably a pair of carpenter's compasses and his ruler divided into nothing smaller than sixteenths of an inch. Converting measurements on a drawing into full-size dimensions should be done by the designer, or it is his own fault if the builder does not build the ship he designed. Moreover copies, whether blue prints or in black and white form, distort in the making and measurements taken off them run the risk of being quite wrong. The original pencil drawing is the most accurate one, and all important measurements not amenable to simple calculation should be taken from this and written on the tracing.

Again, write all letters and figures boldly and large on the drawings. By the time a builder has had them lying about his workshop for a month or two they will be smeared and dusty, and small figures will be easily misread. In any case, some builders can make astonishing mistakes.

86

Do not ink in the completed pencil drawing. It takes no longer to make a tracing of it in Indian ink, and once a tracing is made any numbers of copies can be taken off, either blue prints or black positive photo prints. If the tracing seems difficult, there are firms who specialize in making tracings from the pencil drawings of their clients; but beware mistakes in your original, for every line, right or wrong, is copied.

Besides a drawing-board and T-square the following few instruments are more or less essential to a designer. A pencil of H or HH hardness, and once one has acquired the knack of using it a flat chisel point is to be recommended for ruled lines of any length; lots of india-rubber; a scale or ruler in inches, for calculations one divided into fiftieths is most useful, while for constructional drawings one divided into twelfths and sixteenths is most useful; two set-squares, one large and one small; and finally a pair of dividers. Ship's curves are very helpful in getting smooth curves, or any of the flexible curves and paraphernalia with which drawing-instrument-makers tempt one. Ship's curves are despised by some authorities, but they are very good none the less, and a dozen or more need only cost 1s., the price of some odd pieces of thick celluloid from a garage where they mend side screens. Narrow pieces about 2 feet long cut easily into long sweeping curves of various shapes, which is best done by drawing the curve on a piece of paper, laying the celluloid over it, and tracing the curve with a sharp point scratching the celluloid. Tin snips will cut round this, leaving only a slightly rough edge to be smoothed off with a spokeshave.

Drawing paper is as important as the instruments. Various qualities are available, but in sheets 30 inches by 22 inches called imperial, it is probably the most convenient for amateur use. Tracing paper is much cheaper than tracing cloth and gives equally good prints ; it is only less durable.

A special pen is made for indian ink, with jaws that screw up together and enable the thickness of the line to be adjusted. A mapping pen is not a good thing for ruled lines, though useful for lettering and touching up when need be.

Failing a pretty but expensive instrument called a planimeter, which measures areas by itself, transparent squared paper is the best thing to use. This can be got divided into inches and tenths of an inch.

VIII

CALCULATING AREAS AND VOLUMES

The only bit of theoretical mechanics essential to those who dabble seriously in design of ships is in computing areas between curves and straight lines, and in locating the centre of gravity of an oddly shaped area or volume.

A simple way of finding the area enclosed by a curve is to lay over it a piece of transparent paper divided like graph paper, into squares. The squares enclosed by the curve are then counted. Alternatively one can find the area by applying a formula proved some two hundred years ago by a mathematician called Simpson. He showed that the area between AE and a curve such as FGHKL in fig. 17 (i) is given very nearly by the formula,

$$\text{area} = \frac{AB}{3} \times (AL + 4.BK + 2.CH + 4.DG + EF)$$

where the line AE is divided into equal parts AB, BC, CD, and DE. There may be any odd number of ordinates in AE, the ordinates always being multiplied successively by 4 and 2, except for the end ordinates, which are multiplied by 1.

To apply the formula in general, the line AE is divided into an even number of parts, so giving an odd number of ordinates; and then a table is made up as on page 90, giving:

In Column I the positions of A, B, C, D, and E ;
    II the lengths of the ordinates at these
        positions ;
    III the proper multipliers 1, 4, 2, 4, . . .1,
        for Simpson's area formula ;
    IV the products of figures in Columns II
        and III.

These products as set out in the fourth column are then added up, and the sum multiplied by one-third of the distance between the ordinates, i.e. $\frac{AB}{3}$, which gives the area of the curve. This method is often preferable to using squared paper.

AREA OF FIG. 17 (i)

Column I	Column II	Column III	Column IV
			Products of
		Simpson's	Columns II
Position	Lengths	multipliers	and III
A	3·2	1	3·2
B	5·6	4	22·4
C	6·8	2	13·6
D	6·2	4	24·8
E	2·0	1	2·0

Sum of products in
    column IV . . . 66·0

Spacing AB = 10
    Hence the area between the line A E and the
curve F G H K L is . . . . $\frac{10}{3} \times 66\cdot0$
                   = 220

The centres of gravity of areas and volumes bounded by curves are found by a simple extension of Simpson's rule, and there is no necessity to understand reasons for the steps involved. However, a short digression is given for the satisfaction of those who do not like taking such things on faith. Others can skip it, and find the rule in the last two paragraphs of this section.

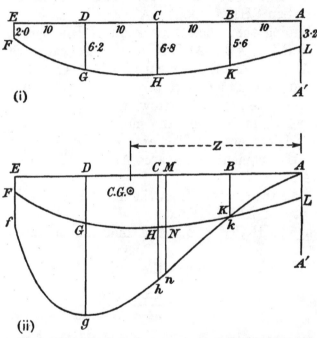

FIG. 17.—Computing areas and locating centre of gravity.

Centre of Gravity calculations involve what are called "moments," and the moment of an area is the area multiplied by the distance from its centre of gravity to a line. Again, an important law of mechanics is that the moment of an area about a line equals the sum of the moments of individual parts of the area about the line.

91

Referring to fig. 17 (ii), CM is supposed very small so that the centre of a very narrow strip CHNM is approximately a distance AC from the line AA'. Thus the moment of the strip is CM × CH × AC. Now mark off C*h* equal to CH × AC, and the area enclosed by C*hn*M is C*h* × CM, which equals the moment of the narrow strip CHNM about AA'.

Continuing the process, mark off at B a length B*k* equal to BK × AB. At D mark off D*g* equal to DG × AD. At E mark off E*f* equal to EF × AE. Draw a curve through A*khgf*, and the area of this curve is made up of the areas of narrow strips corresponding to C*hn*M, which in turn are the moments of small parts of the original curve. The area of A*khgf*E is consequently the moment of the area ALKHGFE about the line AA'.

Let Z be the distance from the line AA' to the centre of gravity of ALKHGFE.

Then ALKHGFE × Z = the moment of the area about AA'.

= the area A*khgf*E.

Hence $$Z = \frac{\text{area } A\textit{khgf}E}{\text{area AKHGFE}}$$

To get the ordinates of curve A*khgf*E the distances of the positions A, B, C, D, and E from the line AA' are required, but since AB is a common multiple of all the distances, multiplication is simplified by using the series 0, 1, 2, 3, . . . to give the second curve ordinates, the actual length AB coming in once only after the summing.

In practice the table already described for areas is continued by a fifth column giving the distance multipliers 0, 1, 2, 3, . . . (whereby the second curve ordinates are derived) and by a sixth column giving the products of columns IV and V (see p. 98). (Note that the result is the same whether the ordinates of column II are multiplied first by the series 1, 4, 2, 4, . . .1, or by the series 0, 1, 2, 3, . . .)

Let the sum of the figures in column VI = P
Let the sum of the figures in column IV = Q

$$\text{then } Z = \frac{P}{Q} \times AB$$

Examples follow in the next section.

Volumes.

In dealing with the volumes of solid things cross-sections are made at equal intervals, and the areas of these cross-sections treated as the ordinates of a straightforward curve ; the area of the curve with these ordinates is the volume of the solid, and the centre of gravity is located as for an area.

Sail Plans.

For the areas and centres of straight-sided figures, such as sails can generally be considered, we make use of the properties of triangles. The first of these is for area.

Calling the three corner points of a triangle, A, B, and C, the area of the triangle ABC is

$\frac{1}{2}$ × BC × *perpendicular* distance from A to BC

a formula worked very hard in measuring sail plans.

Foresails and bermudian mainsails are triangular in shape, and their areas follow readily from the sail plan. (If one side is slightly convex it suffices to draw a straight

93

line through the curve so as to give approximately the same area.)

A gaff mainsail is no more difficult, for by drawing a line from throat to clew the sail is divided into two triangles whose areas can be measured separately and added together.

The centre of effort of the sail plan has been explained on page 48, and to locate it one must first find the centres of gravity of each separate sail ; for which one again turns to the properties of triangles.

To find the centre of gravity of a triangle ABC draw a line from the corner A to the mid-point of the side BC, and another line from the corner B to the mid-point of the side AC. Where these two cross is the centre of gravity.

Triangular sails are easily solved thus, and using a little cunning geometry a gaff sail can be as easily dealt with. On the sail plan draw a line from throat to clew and find the centres of the two triangles so formed. If these points are called W and X respectively, clearly the C.G. of the sail must lie somewhere on the line WX. Now draw a line from peak to tack, and find the centres of the two new triangles so formed. If these positions are Y and Z respectively, clearly the C.G. of the whole sail lies on the line YZ. Where WX and YZ cross is the point sought.

The centre of effort of the whole sail plan can now be located by applying the law of moments (given on page 91) to the various sails comprising it. In fig. 13 imagine a line drawn vertically upwards through the stem-head of one of the boats ; then

call M the area of the mainsail,

call S the area of the staysail,

call J the area of the jib,
call m the perpendicular distance from the C.G. of
M to the vertical through the stem-head,
call s the perpendicular distance from the C.G. of
S to the vertical through the stem-head,
call j the perpendicular distance from the C.G. of
J to the vertical through the stem-head.
The distance from the vertical through the stem-head
to the centre of effort of the whole sail plan is now

$$\frac{M \times m + S \times s + J \times j}{M + S + J}$$

IX

ANALYSIS OF HULL FORM

The Curve of Areas, or Displacement Curve.

The sections of a yacht's hull differ much in shape, and since it is the displaced volume of water that keeps the yacht afloat, it is usual to examine the shape of a yacht's underwater body by means of a curve showing the immersed area at any position on the water line. For this the submerged part of each section is measured for area and a curve drawn through points found by setting off these areas as ordinates on the water line as base. Failing a planimeter these areas are most conveniently measured with a piece of transparent squared paper divided into inches and tenths of an inch. In fig. 16 the immersed part is the part below PQ, so sections 1 and 5 have no immersed area at all. For the other sections the transparent squared paper is laid on the drawing with one horizontal line along PQ and one vertical line along OZ. The squares enclosed by each section contour between OQ (or OP) and OZ are then counted.

With one-inch squares marked by thicker lines this does not take long, as, with the corner of a major square at O, complete inch squares are first counted and only those small squares between the section contour and the nearest enclosed major line are counted individually. Fractions of small squares can be ignored if less than half a small square, and counted as one small square if more than half. Major squares count as units and the small squares as hundredths, and the answer is, of course, in square inches.

The conventional place for this curve of areas is below the half-breadth plan, but on the same axis where the L.W.L. and the section positions are already marked. Any suitable scale can be chosen for this curve, an example of which is found in fig. 3, from which curve one can see how the displacement volume is distributed along the water line.

The Centre of Lateral Resistance.

As explained in the section on sailing and rig, leeway is opposed by water pressure on the side and keel of the hull, and the position of the resultant water pressure is called the centre of lateral resistance, which, for comparative purposes, is assumed to be at the centre of gravity of the area corresponding to LWRTUL in fig. 16.

The centre of gravity of this area is found by using Simpson's rule for areas, a calculation performed on page 98 for the lines of fig. 3.

In Column I is the section position number.

> II is the draft measured between the water line and the bottom of the keel.

> III are Simpson's multipliers.

> IV are the products of the two preceding columns.

> V are the distances from No. 1 Section, measured in units of section spacing, 0, 1, 2, etc.

> VI are the products of columns IV and V.

The distance to the C.L.R. then follows from the rule for z given on page 92.

CALCULATING AREAS AND LOCATING THE CENTRE OF LATERAL RESISTANCE

Scale of drawing, $\frac{1}{4}'' = 1$ ft.
Section spacing $= 1 \cdot 375$ in.

I	II	III	IV	V	VI
Section No.	Draft	Simpson's Numbers	Products	Distance to No. 1	Products
1	0	1	0	0	0
2	0·80	4	3·20	1	3·20
3	1·02	2	2·04	2	4·08
4	1·08	4	4·32	3	12·96
5	0·80	1	0·80	4	3·20
			sum = 10·36		sum = 23·44

$$\text{Area} = 10{\cdot}36 \times \frac{1{\cdot}375}{3} = 4{\cdot}75 \text{ sq. in.}$$

or full size $4{\cdot}75 \times 4^2 = 76$ sq. ft.

Distance from No. 1 Section to Centre of Lateral Resistance

$$\text{(or to Centre of Gravity)} = \frac{23{\cdot}44}{10{\cdot}36} \times 1{\cdot}375 = 3{\cdot}11 \text{ in.}$$

Displacement and Centre of Buoyancy.

The first thing for these calculations is to measure the immersed areas of the sections as done for the curve of areas. Examining the lines of our example ship of fig. 3, the results are set out on page 99.

In Column I are the section position numbers.

II are the half areas of the sections as measured on the drawing.

III the half areas are doubled.

The table and calculations then proceed as for areas.

98

DISPLACEMENT AND CENTRE OF BUOYANCY COMPUTATIONS

Scale of drawing, $\frac{1}{4}'' = 1$ ft.
Section spacing = 1·375 in.

I	II	III	IV	V	VI	VII
Section No.	Half Area	Whole Area	Simpson's Numbers	Products	Distance to No. 1	Products
1	0	0	1	0	0	0
2	0·285	0·57	4	2·28	1	2·28
3	0·485	0·97	2	1·94	2	3·88
4	0·32	0·64	4	2·56	3	7·68
5	0	0	1	0	4	0
				sum = 6·78		sum = 13·84

Displacement $= 6\cdot78 \times \dfrac{1\cdot375}{3} = 3\cdot11$ cub. in.

Full scale displacement $= 3\cdot11 \times 4^3 = 199$ cub. ft.

$$\text{or } \frac{199}{35} = 5\cdot68 \text{ tons.}$$

Distance from Centre of Buoyancy to No. 1 Section

$$= \frac{13\cdot84}{6\cdot78} \times 1\cdot375 = 2\cdot81 \text{ in.}$$

Working things out as before one now gets the complete immersed volume or displacement of the ship and the distance of its centre of gravity from number 1 section. For the lines examined the volume is 3·11 cubic inches, and the distance of its centre of gravity from number 1 section is 2·81 inches.

But what of the real ship? Its volume will be in cubic feet and its centre of buoyancy a matter of feet from number 1 section. The C.B. of the ship is the C.G. of the volume analysed; so to convert the 2·81 inches into full-size dimensions one multiplies by 4, i.e. the scale of the drawing, 4 feet to an inch. For the real volume in cubic feet one has to multiply by the cube of four, i.e. 64, thus,

full-size displacement volume $= 3 \cdot 11 \times 64$
$$= 199 \cdot 04 \text{ cub. ft.}$$

To convert this displacement volume into tons divide by 35 (see page 10), thus,

$$\text{displacement in tons} = \frac{199 \cdot 04}{35} = 5 \cdot 68$$

X

DESIGN RULES AND THEORIES

In this intriguing subject of yacht design one sometimes hears theories as to what is essential to ensure hull perfection, theories that are urged as Gospel although without any experimental evidence in their favour. Very often such ideas are expounded under the title of Balance.

There are, however, two rules of importance in the history of design, one concerning wedges of immersion and emersion, and another called the metacentric shelf system. Both these relate to the heeled position of the yacht, which is not only the normal sailing position but a constantly changing position.

The effect of heeling in squally weather is often discussed, but it is sometimes forgotten that in rough water every wave alters the shape of the immersed part of the hull and that a long beam wave alters the ship's load water-line plane to that of a heeled position, causing changes in shape in the hull's immersed volume regardless of whether the yacht herself heels or not. Fig. 18 should make this clear.

Wedges of Immersion and Emersion.

This widely diffused theory is in effect that a yacht's centre of buoyancy should not move aft if, on heeling, she rotates or pivots about the central axis of her load water line, i.e. about the line LW of fig. 16. Wedges come into it because on heeling a yacht puts a wedge-shaped piece of hull into the water to leeward and takes another wedge-shaped piece out from the windward side.

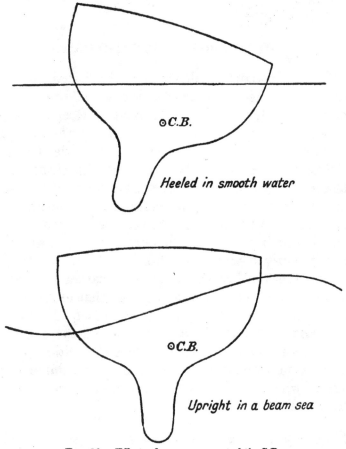

Heeled in smooth water

Upright in a beam sea

FIG. 18.—Effect of waves on a yacht's C.B.

These wedges are rather like slices of melon in shape, extending from bow to stern and being fattest in the middle.

Fig. 19 shows the midship section of a heeled yacht.

102

Upright the water line would be POQ, heeled over it is COD. Using the phraseology usual to the theory, the midship section immerses a wedge POC to leeward and

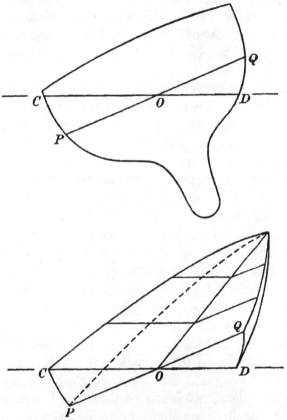

Fig. 19.—Wedges of immersion and emersion.

emerses a wedge QOD to windward. This happens not only to the midship section but all along the hull, so that the two wedges POC and QOD are part of solid slices tapering away to points at either end, as the lower sketch in fig. 19 represents.

It may be that the ingoing wedge volume is bigger abaft the midship section than forward of it, and if such a shape goes into the water clearly it will increase the volume aft more than forward, resulting in a relatively bigger after body when heeled than when upright. The centre of buoyancy of the hull naturally moves in the direction of the biggest increase in volume, so moving aft as the ship rolls.

Just as a piece of wood suspended by a string balances steadily when the centre of gravity lies vertically under the string, so a ship floats steadily if her centre of gravity is vertically below the point through which the resultant upward water pressure acts. This point (the metacentre) is vertically over the centre of buoyancy, and if for any reason the centre of buoyancy moves aft the upward pressure moves aft too and is no longer in line with the ship's centre of gravity. The consequence of such a shift is to make the ship pitch fore and aft in such a way as to bring the centre of buoyancy back into line with the ship's centre of gravity, and it follows that a ship cannot pivot about LW (fig. 16) as axis if the centre of buoyancy moves aft when she does so.

Detrimental consequences of such a movement are sometimes attributed to the fact that a pitching movement in a heeled yacht tilts the keel plane fore and aft, and the keel plane, not being vertical in a heeled yacht, will change its direction slightly and take the yacht with it. How this change of keel plane comes about can be seen by taking a piece of paper to represent the yacht's profile or keel plane, holding it at some 30 degrees to represent the yacht's angle of heel with, say, a table-top to represent the water-level. Tilting the paper forward to represent a pitching movement shows at once

104

that when the paper is tilted to 90 degrees the keel plane has changed direction 30 degrees.

Actually a 90-degree tilt is the impossible situation of a boat standing on her bows, and with a motion such as really occurs the change of keel plane is very small, seldom reaching one degree. Other things are also affecting fore-and-aft trim or tilt, notably wind pressure in the sails and water pressure under the hull, and it is unlikely that the above explanation is correct. Besides, what evidence does the performance of yachts give as to the value of this feature in design ? Certainly many very fast hulls are balanced according to the theory, but equally certainly there are superbly fast hulls utterly unbalanced according to it, for example, *Endeavour I.* In most cruising yachts at any rate some shift of C.B. does occur on heeling, which in normally shaped hulls seldom reaches 1 per cent of the load water line for a 25-degree angle of heel. An average figure for small yachts is about 0·6 per cent of the load water line.

Now as the weight of the hull does not change on heeling, neither does the displaced volume of water (for the hull weight equals the weight of displaced water), and in the foregoing discussion on wedges it has been assumed that the hull rotates about a longitudinal axis through O in fig. 19 without any inquiry as to whether this assumption is reasonable. Such a rotation about O almost invariably makes the ingoing wedge greater than the outcoming wedge, and in reality almost all boats have to rise slightly to keep the displacement volume constant as they heel over.

However, it is the wind that heels the boat, and once it starts to heel there is a downward component on the sails, which increases with the wind and angle of heel;

in consequence it has been pointed out that boats do rotate about an axis not so very far from that through O in fig. 19. In applying the rule in design it makes little difference whether the yacht rotates about O or not, so that one may as well assume that it does so rotate for the sake of the simplification that follows.

Unless in the process of designing a deliberate attempt is made to achieve a stationary centre of buoyancy on heeling, a shift is certain to take place. But yacht

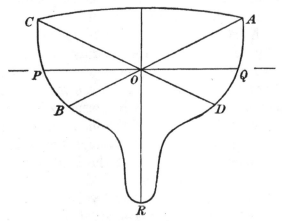

FIG. 20.—Analysis of inclined section.

design is not an exact science. Rules are applied in drawing the lines by a process of trial and error, which means that a designer draws out and analyses a preliminary set of lines, finding out how much they are wrong, and then proceeding to improve them in the direction required ; then he analyses them again. After each analysis the lines are amended slightly until they meet with approval or the designer gets tired.

To obtain a hull faultless as regards shift of centre of buoyancy a preliminary drawing is made and the heeled water lines put in, as at AB and CD on the section drawing of fig. 20. These inclined water lines are put in at an angle to bring the midship gun'les nearly under, generally about 25 degrees. Putting in both the inclined water lines enables the whole heeled shape to be analysed from the half sections drawing, for in fig. 20, showing a complete section, the under-water shape ABRDQA is the same as AORDQA + DORD. The shape of the ingoing wedge is AOQ and of the outcoming wedge DOQ, so that with these two lines AB and CD the heeled form can be analysed with but half a section to work on.

To study the wedges we have to find the volumes and locate the centres of gravity of the ingoing and outcoming wedges as shown on the drawing, and deduce the shift of centre of buoyancy by the formula :

$$\text{Shift of C.B.} = \frac{Ww - Vv - (W - V)d}{D + W - V}$$

where D, W and V are the volumes of hull displacement, ingoing wedge, and outcoming wedge respectively ; and d, w, and v the distances of the C.G.s of these volumes from the fore end of the water line. (The formula itself follows at once on taking moments about the fore end of the water line.)

In this formula D and d are found by the process on page 99 for displacement and centre of buoyancy. The wedge volumes W and V and the distances w and v are found by a similar process, exemplified on page 108 for the lines of fig. 3. The figures and dimensions are for the scale to which the lines are drawn and the processes can be checked up step by step.

For these preliminary lines the C.B. shift may be far

CENTRE OF BUOYANCY SHIFT IN HEELED YACHT

Displacement $D = 3\cdot11$ cub. in.

Distance of Centre of Buoyancy from No. 1 Section $= 2\cdot81$ in.

Section spacing $= 1\cdot375$ in.

(These values were found on page 99.)

INGOING WEDGE

Section No.	Wedge Area	Simpson's Numbers	Products	Distances to No. 1	Products
1	0	1	0	0	0
2	0·15	4	0·60	1	0·60
3	0·26	2	0·52	2	1·04
4	0·22	4	0·88	3	2·64
5	0	1	0	4	0
			sum = 2·00		sum = 4·28

Ingoing wedge volume, $W = 2\cdot00 \times \dfrac{1\cdot375}{3} = 0\cdot916$ cub. in.

Distance of Centre of Gravity from No. 1 Section, w,

$$= \frac{4\cdot28}{2\cdot00} \times 1\cdot375 = 2\cdot94 \text{ in.}$$

OUTCOMING WEDGE

Section No.	Wedge Area	Simpson's Numbers	Products	Distances to No. 1	Products
1	0	1	0	0	0
2	0·09	4	0·36	1	0·36
3	0·18	2	0·36	2	0·72
4	0·12	4	0·48	3	1·44
5	0	1	0	4	0
			sum = 1·20		sum = 2·52

Outcoming wedge volume, $V = 1\cdot20 \times \dfrac{1\cdot375}{3} = 0\cdot55$ cub. in.

Distance of Centre of Gravity from No. 1 Section, v,

$$= \frac{2\cdot52}{1\cdot20} \times 1\cdot375 = 2\cdot89 \text{ in.}$$

Shift of C.B. is $\dfrac{Ww - Vv - (W - V)d}{D - W - V} = 0\cdot023$ in.

$$= 0\cdot42\% \text{ of L.W.L.}$$

from pleasing to the designer, in which event the sections will have to be altered. The C.B. shift of this example is aft, hence abaft the midship section the ingoing wedges are too large or the outcoming wedges too small, and forward of the midship section the ingoing wedges are too small and the outcoming wedges too large. The sections are altered accordingly, by eye at first and then faired up, after which the amended drawing is analysed again for shift of C.B. This time it should be much smaller, though if not small enough yet further amendment will be necessary.

The process just described is applicable to all forms of hull, but where the ingoing wedge is considerably bigger than the outcoming wedge a little time can be saved by using the difference between ingoing and outcoming areas at each section. For this short cut ingoing and outcoming areas at each section are put into adjacent columns and the difference between them in a third column, after which we carry on as before. The first summation multiplied by $\dfrac{l}{3}$ (l being the section spacing) naturally gives the volume $W - V$; and the last column summation multiplied by $\dfrac{l^2}{3}$ gives the moment of this volume about No. 1 section (see page 92). But by first principles this equals the sum of moments of individual parts about number 1 section, i.e. $Ww - Vv$, and thus with only one set of calculations we get $W - V$ and $Ww - Vv$.

On p. 110 the example on p. 108 is worked out thus:

SHORT CUT IN C.B. CALCULATIONS

Section No.	Ingoing Area	Outcoming Area	Difference	Simpson's Numbers	Products	Distances to No. 1	Products
1	0	0	0	1	0	0	0
2	0·15	0·09	0·06	4	0·24	1	0·24
3	0·26	0·18	0·08	2	0·16	2	0·32
4	0·22	0·12	0·10	4	0·40	3	1·20
5	0	0	0	1	0	4	0
					sum = 0·80		sum = 1·76

Hence $W - V = 0\cdot80 \times \dfrac{1\cdot375}{3} = 0\cdot366$

and $Ww - Vv = 1\cdot76 \times \dfrac{(1\cdot375)^2}{3} = 1\cdot11$

The Metacentric Shelf System.

The metacentric shelf theory of hull form is an important new-comer. Besides a foundation of considerable theoretical reasoning it has the support of those who have seriously experimented with it both in the model yacht world and with the real thing.

A yacht's hull is a strangely shaped thing when upright; but when heeled over even the axis of symmetry along the centre line disappears from the immersed part, which becomes a hopelessly irregular shape. Engineer Rear-Admiral Turner originated the idea of getting some form of regularity into this curiously shaped thing, and his term "Metacentric Shelf" is an imposing name for a simple line of points of mathematical significance, which line does duty for an axis of symmetry in the submerged part of the hull.

To understand the theory further one must think out what happens to the submerged part of a hull as the ship heels over. The important part is the centre of buoyancy, the C.B., which is the centre of gravity of the immersed volume. As the ship heels this C.B. moves sideways owing to the changing shape of the immersed part of the hull; in fig. 21 it moves from B_1 when upright to some position such as B_2 when heeled. Thinking for the moment of the upright position there is a point on the central axis which is vertically above the C.B. both when upright and heeled. Such a point is shown at M_1 in fig. 21, with the ship's C.B. vertically beneath it at B_1. If now the ship heels a small amount, say 2 or 3 degrees only, M_1 will heel round with the ship to the position M_2, while the C.B. will move sideways to some position B_2, vertically below M_2. So far as the

111

hull is concerned, M_2 is the same point as M_1, and this point M_2 is called the transverse metacentre of the ship, and the length B_1M_1 the metacentric height. If, however, the ship heels considerably, some 20 degrees or so, the metacentre itself moves somewhat relative to the ship and the C.B. may be found at some point B_3.

The first metacentric rule is that even for large angles of heel the position of the heeled C.B. must be under

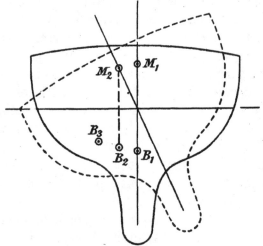

FIG. 21.—Metacentric balance.

M_2, i.e. as shown at B_2. If it moves to B_3 the hull is not perfectly balanced.

The second and most important part of the rule deals with individual sections. Fig. 22 shows both the vertical and heeled sections of a hull, and their positions relative to the water-level. Thinking of these sections as thin slices, each immersed part will have a C.B. at its centre of gravity. Upright these centres of buoyancy lie naturally on the vertical axis of symmetry as shown

H

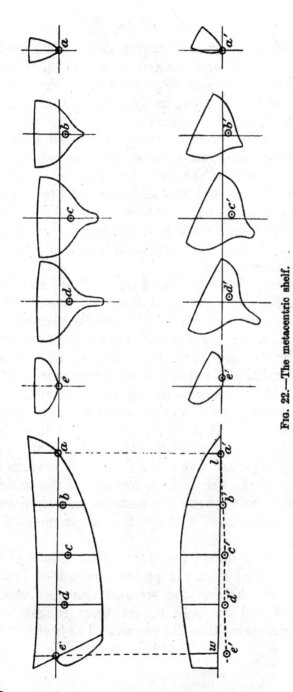

FIG. 22.—The metacentric shelf.

at *a*, *b*, *c*, *d*, and *e*, in the drawing showing the vertical
positions. Heeled over the centres of buoyancy move
to the right by an amount depending on the shape of the
sections ; and at any one section the C.B. may move
more or less than at the next section on the drawing.
Such heeled centres of buoyancy are shown at *a'*, *b'*,
c', *d'*, and *e'* on the drawing showing the heeled sections.

At the fore end of the water line the C.B. at *a'* has
not moved at all, but as the immersed area of this
section is nothing it need not trouble us. At the stern
the water line itself may have extended slightly, but
the immersed areas here are small and their effect of
no importance either.

Transferring the positions of *a'*, *b'*, *c'*, *d'*, and *e'* on
to the half-breadth plan will show the movement at
each section, and a line on the half-breadth plan through
a', *b'*, *c'*, *d'*, and *e'* gives what is called the Metacentric
Shelf. Such a line is shown dotted in fig. 22, and
metacentric balance requires this metacentric shelf to
be a straight line parallel to the ship's centre line *lw*,
or if not straight to lie evenly about a mean position
running fore and aft parallel to the centre line. The
shelf in fig. 22 does not fulfil this requirement.

In many ships the curve *a' b' c' d' e'* bends towards the
centre line of the ship a little forward of the midship
section, and abaft the midship section bends right away
from the centre line, a shape that is pronounced in
ships that gripe.

To produce a design fulfilling the conditions of the
metacentric shelf theory a preliminary set of lines is
drawn, a set showing the sections and just enough
water lines and buttocks to get them roughly fair.
Fig. 23 then exemplifies the process. The heeled water

lines AB and CD are drawn in, and the shape of each under-water heeled section copied on to a piece of thin flat paper by the simple process of tracing. Thin typing paper is quite satisfactory for this purpose.

(1) Beginning with number 3 section lay on the paper and rule in AB and OT. Trace in the side AQDT. Then turn the tracing paper over and lay it on the drawing with OT as before but with the traced line AB along CD. Now trace in the line DT, and this will complete the section.

This tracing business is done for each section using a separate sheet of paper for each one. No. 4 half section is on the left of the central axis and with AB as the water line the small piece BS is drawn first, followed by CPBS when the tracing paper is turned over. Finally, these heeled section tracings are cut out with scissors giving the shapes shown in fig. 23 (i), (ii) and (iii).

All these cut-out sections need a line OV at right angles to the water line AB, and if this is put in on the original drawing it is no trouble to trace it with the other lines.

Having cut out the sections, there are three things yet to complete the analysis. (1) Balance each section separately on a knife-edge with the line OV parallel to the blade of the knife; mark the paper where the knife-edge comes and draw a line immediately over it, i.e. parallel to OV. These lines are shown as K_3E, K_3E, and K_4E, in fig. 23 (i) (ii) and (iii), the subscript numbers denoting the section.

All this is in pursuit of the centres of buoyancy of the heeled sections, centres whose position is now settled by the lines KE, at any rate from a vertical viewpoint.

Looking down on the half-breadth plan of the drawing the heeled centres of buoyancy are to one side of the axis by distances OK_2, OK_3 and OK_4.

The end section No. 5 is a minor problem. At 25 degrees as drawn the heeled area is practically nothing but a line ; at greater angles it would become a definite area, while at lesser angles it would have no immersed area at all. The centre of buoyancy of such immersed area as exists at 25 degrees is shown at K_5 on the half-breadth plan, but for smaller angles it would be put in on the centre line. At number 1 section no area is immersed on heeling and the centre of buoyancy is put in on the axis at K_1. The two points K_1 and K_5 end off the theoretical metacentric shelf curve, and with these two end points corresponding to sections 1 and 5 we can draw a curve through K_1, K_2, K_3, K_4, and K_5, and this curve is the Metacentric Shelf for the boat. In an actual drawing five sections would be insufficient and at least twelve are required for any degree of accuracy.

(2) Stick all the paper sections together, using only a touch of gum to each, and stick them so that all the edges AB come together one above the other, and all the lines OV come one over the other (see fig. 23 (iv)). When dry balance this bunch on a knife-edge, and as before measure the distance OK from the knife-edge to the line OV. Mark this distance off anywhere below the line lw in the half-breadth plan, so getting a point as at K ; and through K draw KN parallel to lw.

The metacentric shelf found by process (1) will lie close to this line KN, possibly coincident with it but more probably lying across it or curving about it, and

116

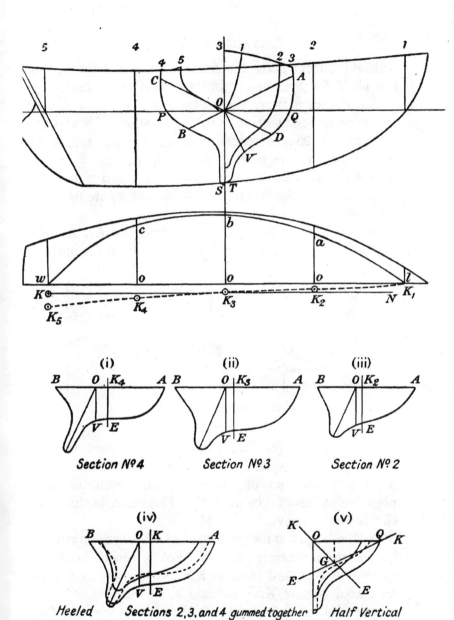

FIG. 23.—Process of metacentric shelf analysis.

117

Admiral Turner gives the following method for testing the shelf for symmetry and freedom from faults.

The distance from the metacentric shelf to KN is measured at each section. In fig. 24, where KN and the shelf of fig. 23 are redrawn on an exaggerated scale, these distances are marked d_1, d_2, d_3, d_4, and d_5. Distances d_1, d_2, and d_3 are considered positive because they are above the line KN, while d_4, and d_5 are negative because they are below the line.

Let the heeled areas of the sections be A_1, A_2, A_3, A_4, and A_5. Then at section 1 mark off an ordinate of

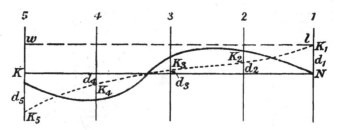

FIG. 24.—Test of a metacentric shelf.

height $A_1 \times d_1$ (in this example it is zero because $A_1 = 0$). At section 2 mark off an ordinate of height $A_2 \times d_2$. And so on, marking off ordinates with negative values of d below KN. This curve is shown by the full line curve in fig. 24.

With a large number of sections this curve is naturally far more accurately drawn. For a good boat the curve will be found to cross KN twice, showing a negative area (below KN) amidships, and a positive area (above KN) at either end. If the shelf is without fault the two positive areas (above KN) will be equal.

It may be noted that these two areas above KN

118

should together be equal to the area below KN, for the curve's total area is the moment about the C.G., which moment is always zero.

(3) Here some mathematics are necessary in settling the position of the transverse metacentre, M_1 in fig. 21.

The C.B. position B_1 can be found by a means to be described, and from this the point M_1 is fixed, for it can be proved that the distance $B_1M_1 = \dfrac{I}{V}$, where I is a quantity known as the moment of inertia of the water-line plane about the axis, and V is the displacement volume.

To find I the half breadths of the water line, oa, ob, and oc in fig. 23, are measured and their values cubed. These cubes are now tabled and multiplied by Simpson's numbers exactly as though they were ordinates of a curve whose area is required, see page 120, where the half breadths actually shown are those of fig. 3.

Let H be the pseudo-area resulting, i.e. the sum of the products multiplied by one-third of the section spacing ;

$$\text{then } I = \frac{2}{3} \times H$$

The displacement volume V is determined as before, and B_1M_1 is then quickly found.

The gummed sections have now to be cut up, so, as they cannot be verified without cutting out a new set of sections, the preceding measurements need careful checking stage by stage. Cut away from the gummed bunch of sections the parts corresponding to AOQ and BOT of fig. 23 (top), so leaving the original half sections

COMPUTING THE METACENTRIC HEIGHT

Section No.	L.W.L. Half Breadths	Cubes	Simpson's Numbers	Products
1	0·0	0	1	0
2	0·72	0·37	4	1·48
3	1·01	1·03	2	2·06
4	0·88	0·68	4	2·72
5	0·06	0·00	1	0

$$\text{sum} = 6·26$$

Section spacing = 1·375 in.

Therefore $H = 6·26 \times \dfrac{1·375}{3} = 2·87.$

Moment of inertia, $I = \dfrac{2}{3} H = 1·91.$

Displacement volume, $V = 3·11$ (cub. in.).

Hence, substituting in the formula $B_1M_1 = \dfrac{I}{V}$,

$$\text{distance } B_1M_1 = \dfrac{1·91}{3·11} = 0·62 \text{ in.}$$

all together in a bunch, fig. 23 (v). Find the centre of gravity of this as before by balancing on a knife-edge, but doing it twice with the edge approximately at right angles giving the two lines KE in (v). The exact position of the centre of gravity is where the two lines cross as shown at G.

Measure the perpendicular distance from OQ to G, shown dotted, and mark this off as OG on the centre line of fig. 25, where the sections are redrawn to avoid

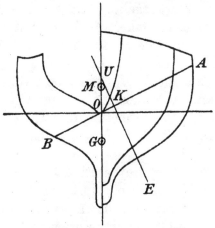

FIG. 25.—Final stage in metacentric analysis.

confusion. This G is the position of the centre of buoyancy of the whole hull when upright.

On this half-section drawing mark off the distance GM equal to B_1M_1 as found above, giving M the transverse metacentre of the hull. Draw the line KE in the position found for the bunch of heeled sections of fig. 23 (iv), and continue this line to cross the central axis at U. This line KE, it will be remembered, is at right angles to AB.

The analysis of the preliminary drawing is now

complete. Is it balanced according to the metacentric theory ?

Process (1) gives the shelf, and if balanced this will be a straight line except at the very ends, or else a line curving evenly about the line KN found by process (2). Process (3) gives the metacentre M, and if balanced the point U in fig. 25 will lie atop M.

Clearly the lines of fig. 3 are wrong on all counts, and we must start again ; but we now know what sort of alterations to make. In fig. 25, KE for the bunch of sections lies outside M, so that in (iv) the average value of OK is too big. If we are trying to get a straight line metacentric shelf, OK_4 must be reduced and OK_2 increased ; and to reduce the average OK to meet the condition of (3) the reduction of OK_4 must be more than the increase of OK_2. It will probably be necessary to reduce OK_3 also.

To increase OK at any section the section must be altered either by filling out just above the water line or by cutting away low down in the section. Conversely to reduce OK at any section the shape must be altered by reducing the area just above the water line or by increasing the draft and low-down area of the section.

A second attempt at a preliminary drawing should not be far out, and its touching up a simple matter. After this the lines are completed round the corrected sections and the whole lot analysed. More correction will be necessary here ; but it is tedious rather than difficult to get a perfectly designed hull.

XI

MISCELLANEOUS NOTES

Thames Measurement of Size

A very frequently encountered method of assessing a yacht's size is by "Thames Measurement." For this the ship is measured (1) for length between the stem-head and sternpost at deck-level, L in fig. 26 ; and (2) for maximum beam, B. The Thames Measure-

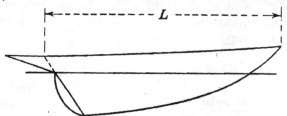

FIG. 26.—Length for Thames Measurement.

ment tonnage is then given by putting these dimensions in the formula,

$$\text{T.M. tonnage} = \frac{(L - B) \times B^2}{188}.$$

This has the advantage of being quick to apply and easy to work out, but it should be treated with caution as a measure of real size. For a modern yacht the formula generally gives a tonnage figure considerably exceeding the displacement tonnage.

Weight and Strength of Materials

From the drawings and specifications one can estimate the cubic feet of the various parts of a yacht, keel, planking, beams, etc., and then from the following

table one can get the weight of the parts and so arrive
at the weight of the whole yacht. One should note
that the weight of timber increases appreciably after
prolonged immersion, and the effect of painting is to
retard, but not to prevent, absorption of water.

The breaking load of a material is the load that would
pull out and break a rod of one square inch section.
Normally metals and timber are permanently distorted
long before this load is reached, and the safe working
load is taken as less than the breaking load by some
five or six times. Timber, however, seldom breaks
down owing to a direct pull, and generally gives way
first where a bolt or rivet passes through it, securing,
for instance, the chain plates to the topsides and transferring the pull of the shrouds to the hull.

WEIGHT AND STRENGTH OF MATERIALS

Material	Weight of One Cubic Foot Pounds	Breaking Load per sq. in. Tons
Sea Water	64	—
Cast Iron	450	8
Mild Steel	490	28
Copper, rolled	550	15
Brass	525	11
Gunmetal	540	15
Lead	710	1
Teak, East Indian	48	6·7
Mahogany, Honduras	35	—
Oak	52	6·2
Elm, English	36	4·3
„ American	45	—
Pitch Pine	48	3·2
Red Deal (joinery)	36	3
Spruce	28	2·9

FOR ADDITIONAL NOTES

INDEX

127